CONTENTS

KU-228-769

MEET THE COACH

Richard White is a sales coach and trainer for trusted advisers specializing in advanced consultative selling skills. Since 2002 Richard has helped many thousands of people become more effective at all aspects of consultative selling from lead generation to closing the sale and developing key accounts.

Richard is a Certified Master NLP Coach and has applied his coaching skills specifically to helping others improve their sales performance while feeling more motivated and confident. Passionate about accelerated learning, he has developed many methodologies for achieving fast change in sales performance.

Richard is known as The Accidental Salesman® and is proof that you do not need to be a born salesperson to be successful in sales. He worked as a business intelligence consultant for over ten years working for Oracle before going on to build a successful consulting practice for an Oracle partner.

You can contact Richard at rwhite@theaccidentalsalesman.com

HOW TO USE THIS BOOK

The objective of this workbook is to enable you to improve the results you get from your current sales activity. I will be coaching you in a similar way to how I might do if we were working together. I am therefore assuming that you are not a complete beginner to sales and you are already engaged in sales activity on a daily basis, even if it is alongside other activities. It is not essential that you have had any formal sales training or have read any other books on sales. It is important, however, to realize that, unless you are engaged in sales activity on a daily basis, you will find it difficult to do the exercises in the coaching sessions.

This workbook has been designed for anyone who wants to improve their consultative selling skills, including:

- sales professionals
- business developers
- business owners
- professionals
- anyone else who has to engage in business-to-business sales on a daily basis.

I have used some collective nouns throughout the workbook to simplify the text. When I refer to 'salespeople' I mean anyone in the above list, even though many business developers, business owners and professionals do not like to admit that they are involved in sales activity. If this is you, then please bear with me and hopefully by the time you complete the book you will feel more comfortable about sales. You will find that the style of selling is very respectful and conducive to developing trusted relationships.

Another term I use throughout the workbook is 'customers', recognizing that many people involved in sales activity prefer to use the term 'client'. I also refer regularly to the term 'products and services', which includes the combination of products and services into a 'solution' or 'package'.

There are several different styles of selling and with all styles of selling there are many similarities but some fundamental differences. The style of selling we will be covering in this workbook is known as 'consultative selling' and specifically in the context of business-to-business sales, although if you are engaged in consultative selling on a business-to-consumer basis much of the book will still apply to you.

THE STRUCTURE OF THIS WORKBOOK

This is a self-coaching workbook and I have divided it into three sections based on my experience of working with experienced salespeople who are looking to achieve improved sales results:

- Part 1: Generating more sales leads
- Part 2: Closing the sale
- Part 3: Becoming more effective at some other aspect of sales performance such as motivation or time management

I do not expect you to complete the whole workbook in one go. Instead, I hope you will start at the part covering the area where you need most help. Whichever part you choose, please do the chapters in that section in order. I have tried to make each chapter as self-contained as possible, but you will gain the biggest benefit by working through in sequence. For example, in Part 2, the first chapter is about sales process and you may be thinking that you understand all about sales process and so there is no need to do that chapter. Yet if you want to get better at closing sales, you need to take a step back and examine your sales process in more detail. Because you are already experienced, the improvements will come from small refinements.

As you are working through a chapter, please keep your focus on the coaching sessions and not the text. The text is there to provide just enough essential information for you to confirm your understanding and then do the exercises.

Part 1 – Generating sales leads

Putting aside issues of motivation, confidence and time management, which are dealt with in Part 3 on sales performance, the reason my coaching clients struggle to generate enough sales leads is rarely to do with technique and more to do with clarity: clarity about who they should be targeting and what they should be saying to generate interest. In other words, it's about identifying a target audience and developing compelling sales messages that your target audience will find attractive. As you work your way through this section, you will be focusing on a specific product or service.

1 Clarifying your target audience

In this chapter you will take a step back and look at what makes an ideal customer for what you are selling. When you have a nice clear definition of your target audience, it makes it easier to understand why they will be interested in buying your products and services. In other words, we will be defining *who* you should be targeting. This will enable you to be more focused. Given all the people

I have coached on lead generation over the last 12 years, I do not recall ever recommending someone to be less focused!

2 Finding the pain

Once we know who your ideal customers are, we then need to look at *why* they might want to talk to you about a specific product or service. In this chapter we look at the pain your customers and prospects are facing and explore the various motives for them wanting to talk to you about that product or service.

3 Your USP

This chapter is about discovering *what* aspects of a specific product or service you should be emphasizing when seeking to generate sales leads. We look at the various features and benefits of your specific product or service – not only what makes it different but also what features will most appeal to your target audience.

4 Crafting your messages

In this chapter we look at the specific words you use to generate interest from your ideal customers. We will be taking all the insights gained from preceding chapters and using them to build a messaging framework from which you will begin to craft your pitch. Additionally, you will learn how to craft a soft pitch for situations where a regular sales pitch is not appropriate.

5 Generating interest

Now that we have the words that will generate interest in your specific product or service, we explore various sources of leads, other than cold calling, that are within your own control as a salesperson.

6 Cold calling

This final chapter looks at how to increase your confidence and effectiveness in cold calling and specifically in the area of scripting.

Part 2 – Closing the sale

In Part 2 we focus on taking an expression of interest in our product or service and converting that interest into a sale. Although you may be tempted to jump straight to this section, please do Part 1 first unless you have a regular stream of sales leads and a clear understanding of your ideal audience and the USP of the product or service you are working on.

7 The process of selling

In this chapter we look at improving the overall process of converting an expression of interest into a sale. We look at the various stages of the process and in particular the qualification stage.

8 Discovering needs and wants

One of the most critical parts of the sales process is the discovery meeting. It also happens to be the stage where there is significant scope for improving sales conversion rates. We cover the four essential elements you need to discover during your sales meetings.

9 Questioning and listening

The two essential skills for being effective at the discovery stage of the sales process are questioning and listening and in this chapter we look at how to improve the quality of information you get so that you are better able to close the sale.

10 Making your proposals more compelling

In consultative selling, the sales proposal is a key selling document and in this chapter you will be working on ensuring that you avoid the common pitfalls so that your proposals have more impact, especially if you have not managed to speak to everyone involved in making the decision.

11 Concluding the sale

This chapter is about what happens once you have delivered your sales proposal and the steps you need to take in order to close more sales and, in particular, how to handle objections.

12 Handling complex sales opportunities

In this chapter we look at what is sometimes referred to as 'complex' sales, where the decision-making process involves more than one person. This is especially relevant if you sell to larger organizations but could equally apply to small and medium-sized businesses.

Part 3 – Improving sales effectiveness

This section is for when you are already generating a constant stream of sales leads and you are happy with your selling skills but still want to improve your sales performance. Alternatively, this section could be for when you think that things like your personal motivation or the way you manage your time are getting in the way of your generating interest or closing a sale. There are a variety of topics, all focused on helping you be more effective in your sales activity.

13 Your motive for action

In this chapter you will develop compelling personal goals that will motivate you to improve your sales performance. You will also learn a technique for bringing your goals to life and taking your personal motivation to a whole new level.

14 Managing your emotions

This chapter is about taking charge of your emotions so that you have fewer negative emotions and more empowering emotions as you engage in your daily sales activity. You learn techniques that will keep you motivated and help you boost your confidence levels for sales meetings and when you need to make formal sales presentations.

15 Developing a mindset for sales success

In this chapter we will be challenging some of your beliefs and assumptions that could be affecting your sales performance.

16 Prioritizing your sales activity

In this chapter you will be looking at how, specifically, you spend your selling time and learning ways to get more sales in less time, including prioritizing the time you spend with existing customers.

17 Improving your skill with people

Sales is a people game and this chapter is about improving the way in which you interact and communicate with people.

 ONLINE RESOURCE

Coach's tips

Throughout this book you'll find boxes like this one inviting you to download materials from the Teach Yourself 'Coach' site. Here, to begin with, is a list of useful coach's tips that you can refer to as you work through the chapters. Go to:

www.TYCoachbooks.com/Sales

Where to begin

Unless you already know, the following sales coaching diagnostic will help you decide which section of this workbook you should start off with.

COACHING SESSION 1

The sales coaching diagnostic

To complete the sales coaching diagnostic, read each statement and then consider how true it is for you. Score yourself as follows:

Score	Meaning
5	The statement is always true for me.
4	The statement is mostly true for me.
3	The statement is true some of the time.
2	The statement is rarely true for me.
1	The statement in never true for me.

Once you have scored each statement, total up your score for each sales focus area.

Part		Score (1–5)
One	I can clearly articulate the qualities of an ideal customer for my products and services.	
	I understand why my ideal customers buy my products and services.	
	I have a clearly defined USP which is based on the benefits my ideal customers get.	
	I have a pitch that is effective at generating interest from my target audience.	
	I am good at getting referrals from my customers and contacts.	
	TOTAL	
Two	I follow a structured sales process and take care to filter out poor-quality sales opportunities.	
	In my sales meetings, my prospective customers tell me why they are going to buy from me.	
	My sales meetings provide me with all the information I need to write a compelling sales proposal.	
	My proposals are compelling and persuasive even to people who have not been involved in the sales process.	
	I manage objections effectively and rarely get price objections.	
	TOTAL	

Three	I have personal goals that motivate me to want to improve my sales performance.	
	I am always calm and confident in sales situations, even when things are not going my way.	
	I regularly challenge assumptions and limiting beliefs that could be affecting my sales performance.	
	I pay attention to how I spend my selling time and I am always looking for ways to maximize the sales I get from the time I invest.	
	I consciously and continually work on improving my interpersonal and communication skills.	
	TOTAL	

DEVELOPING YOUR SELF-COACHING PLAN

Now that you have completed the sales coaching diagnostic, it is time to create your self-coaching plan. You should start working through this book in order of the score for each part, starting with the section with the lowest score.

If your scores for each section are the same, then prioritize them in the following order:

1. Part 3 – Sales effectiveness
2. Part 1 – Lead generation
3. Part 2 – Lead conversion

Now start working through each chapter of the section. At the start of each chapter you will find a self-assessment, which you should complete before starting to work through the coaching sessions. Once you have completed the chapter, repeat the self-assessment and if you get less than 4 then I encourage you to repeat the chapter before proceeding, paying closer attention to the text.

In terms of fitting it into your busy day, all it takes is 15 to 30 minutes of your attention at the start or end of each day. Use this time to work your way through the book and consider how you are going to implement what you have just learned. At the weekends, reflect on what you have done well during the week and what you will do differently the following week.

If you have a sales manager, coach or mentor, then get them involved and share your progress with them. Make sure they hold you to account for making progress so that you persevere, especially when you think you are too busy to work on your skills.

Before you finish this workbook, I encourage you to go through the remaining chapters even if you have achieved a high score in the sales coaching diagnostic above. The issue is that we don't know what we don't know and I find that most salespeople, no matter what level of performance they are currently at, still have the capacity to do even better.

Finally, make sure that you put what you learn into practice because, at the end of the day, it is action that produces sales results. Good luck and happy selling!

Richard White

PART 1
GENERATING SALES LEADS

1 CLARIFYING YOUR TARGET AUDIENCE

✔ OUTCOMES FROM THIS CHAPTER

- Be able to tell the difference between sales leads and sales opportunities
- Take a more targeted approach to sales lead generation
- Know how to profile your ideal customers

COACHING SESSION 2

Self-assessment

For each of the following statements score yourself between 1 and 5. A score of 5 means that this statement is totally true; 1 means that this statement is totally untrue.

Assessment criteria	Score
I understand where lead generation fits within the sales process.	
I focus my lead generation activity on a specific target audience.	
I focus my lead generation efforts on attracting ideal customers.	
I can clearly articulate to other people what makes an ideal customer for me.	
I can tell the difference between a prospect that will make an ideal customer and one that will waste my time and cause me grief.	
TOTAL	

Total up your score. The maximum is 25 out of 25. Even if you give yourself a full score, I recommend that you complete this chapter.

IT ALL STARTS WITH A SALES LEAD

In my work as a sales coach, I regularly meet salespeople who think they have a problem with closing a sale. Yet, when we take a closer look, we discover that they actually have a sales lead problem. They typically are not generating enough sales leads of the right quality to achieve their personal sales targets.

Before going into more detail, I would like to clarify what a sales lead is and where it fits into the overall sales process. Once you have completed this book, you will be taking every sale through some variation of the following seven stages:

1. Generate interest.

2. Qualify interest.

3. Discover wants and needs.

4. Propose your solution.

5. Agree your solution.

6. Conclude the sale.

7. Deliver your solution.

For the purposes of this book, I am defining a sales lead as an expression of interest in your products and services and as such it is the very first stage in the sales process. An expression of interest could be anything from a potential customer who has fully researched their needs and is ready to buy, all the way through to a potential customer who has a problem and is in research mode. We will look at the sales process in more detail in the second section of this book. For now, it is worth saying that a sales lead only becomes a sales opportunity once you have been through an initial filtering process, known in sales parlance as 'qualification'.

As we progress through this section of the book it will become clearer what those wants and needs are and how to get people to want to have such conversations.

TARGETED SALES LEAD GENERATION

Given that we are seeking to generate interest in having sales conversations, the important question is 'How do we generate that interest?'

To be able to answer that question, we need to ask another question: which people, specifically? This is because although there may be many people in the market for what you are selling, they are not all looking for exactly the same things. However, there may be groups of people looking for similar things to each other. It is hard to get people's attention these days, especially with so many other businesses offering similar products and services to the same people. When we are just saying the same things as all our competitors, our message gets lost in the noise. However, when our message is different and highly targeted to the needs and wants of our ideal customers, then it is more likely to get noticed and resonate with them. In short, we begin to stand out from the crowd and get heard by the people who are important to us.

Focusing on a target audience is much more effective because it makes it easier to craft and deliver clear and compelling messages that attract the attention of our ideal customers and stimulate their interest in talking to us about our products and services. The more we understand *who* we want to attract, the easier it is to understand *why* they might like to talk to us and *what* they might find attractive. This in turn will help us define *what* to say that will interest them and *how* to ensure that our ideal customers get to hear our message. As you can see, it all starts with understanding your target audience.

The other important benefit of taking a targeted approach is that when you focus your energy, you get much better results for the energy you put in. If you have two distinct target audiences, it is better to do one at a time and maximize the impact rather than trying to do them both concurrently and dissipating your energy. It's a bit like taking sunlight and passing it through a magnifying glass.

WHO ARE YOUR IDEAL CUSTOMERS?

When seeking to understand where to focus your lead generation activity, a good place to start is by understanding more about your existing customers. When you are looking for more customers willing to buy your products and services, you can gain valuable insights from your existing customers. If you are like most people I have coached in sales, there will be some customers who are more valuable than others and have an especially good fit with your business. They will typically value what you do, buy from you again and again, and refer you to their contacts. From now on I will refer to these as your ideal customers.

If you are going to focus on attracting more new customers, does it not make sense to seek out your ideal customers? When you do, your lead generation efforts will take less time and effort. The sale will be easier to win and, as they will be buying from you regularly and referring you to their contacts, lead generation will also become increasingly easier. When you focus on attracting your ideal customers your messaging will be targeted on those people even though you may still end up attracting potential customers who do not fit 100 per cent with your profile of an ideal customer.

YOUR BEST CUSTOMERS

I now would like you to start thinking about your best customers and when you do I would like you to limit this, if possible, to real customers – people who have paid you money for your products and services. While your relationship is important, it needs to be a commercial relationship where some kind of trading has taken place. If you have provided services for free but your customer has given you a case study, then that could count as a trade but, given that we are seeking to sell our products and services for money, it is best to focus on these people for this coaching session.

If you do not have any relevant customers, either current or previous, then you will need to do some more detailed market research before proceeding.

⍾⍾ COACHING SESSION 3

My best customer

One way to make it easier to clarify your ideal customers is to contrast them with what I call your 'customers from hell'! These are your worst customers and the ones that are not good for business.

If you do not have any current experiences of a customer from hell, then think about previous customers that have been troublesome. Then think about your best customer. Fill in the spaces below.

My worst customer

Name of person	
Name of organization	
What makes this your worst customer?	

My best customer

Name of person	
Name of organization	
What makes this your best customer?	

What we are aiming for is to be crystal clear about what makes an ideal customer for you so that we can begin to understand how to generate their interest in having a sales conversation with us.

5 Star customers

Many websites these days give you the opportunity to rate products and suppliers. For example, on Amazon you can rate products you have purchased and on eBay you can rate suppliers. Typically when rating things online, we are asked to give between 1 and 5 stars to indicate our approval.

What if you were able to rate your existing customers? Which ones would get five stars? Which would get just one star? Would any of your customers get no stars at all? And more importantly, for the purposes of understanding an ideal customer, how do we decide how many stars to give each customer?

I am now going to take you through a process of rating your customers and by the end of the process you will be able to see what an ideal customer looks like. You may even find that, as a result of going through this process, your perception of an ideal customer may change.

We will define the qualities that your ideal customers must possess, and each of the qualities will be worth one star. You will award your customers one star for each of the five qualities they have. Your customers that have all five of the qualities will be your 5 Star customers!

It may seem quite a simplistic exercise but I encourage you to do it thoroughly as the insights gained will form the basis of the remainder of this section and Part 2 of this book.

Example

dmClub is a UK-based company providing simple and affordable telephony services to small businesses. The qualities of dmClub's 5 Star customers are:

- They have fewer than ten employees.
- They are focused on sales growth.
- They care about their image.
- They are very busy.
- They are out of the office a lot.

The first quality is always the one that is non-negotiable, meaning that they would need to have this quality to become a customer. In dmClub's case, they serve the very small business market and although their products and services would work for businesses with more than ten employees, it would not be a very good fit. This is largely because of the way in which dmClub conduct their business and because their products and services are designed for people who are very mobile rather than being office based.

COACHING SESSION 4

Step 1: List all the qualities of your ideal customers

List as many qualities you can think of – aim for at least 20. For example:

- Do they need to be based in a particular location?
- Do they need to have a certain sales revenue or number of employees?
- Do they need to be male or female or does that not matter?
- Are they in a particular job, such as a finance director or marketing director?
- Do they need to be a particular age?

As you do this exercise, think about your best customers and their qualities. Do this quickly without too much thought and analysis. Just list them down and you will be able to judge later.

Qualities

1. _____
2. _____
3. _____
4. _____
5. _____
6. _____
7. _____
8. _____
9. _____
10. _____

11. _____
12. _____
13. _____
14. _____
15. _____
16. _____
17. _____
18. _____
19. _____
20. _____

Step 2: Select the non-negotiable customer quality

Although we will be seeking customers with all five qualities, we will not turn away customers who fail to tick all five boxes. However, we need to have at least one quality that is non-negotiable and without that quality you will turn them away. What quality would it be for you?

Would the customer need to be in a specific location? Would they need to be a certain size of business?

Select your non-negotiable quality and why it is non-negotiable. This quality, like the rest, should be specific and easily verified. However, before you do this, it is worth saying something here about budget. You should be looking for customers that are going to be buying again and again from you rather than making a single purchase, just like your best customers. I normally leave financial elements out of the 5 Star qualities, and especially a budget for what you are trying to sell. If you do want to include something financial, I would encourage you to think about annual budget. For example, while your typical first sale may be £2,000 you may find that your ideal customers have an annual budget of at least £20,000 for what you offer.

My non-negotiable quality: _____

Why it is non-negotiable: _____

Now that you have your first and most important of your 5 Star Customer qualities, it is time to work out the other four.

Step 3: List your remaining top four customer qualities

Now enter the non-negotiable quality as number 1 in the list below and then select the four most important qualities from your list above and add them to this list.

My 5 Star customer qualities

1. _____

2. _____

3. _____

4. _____

5. _____

Step 4: Prioritize your 5 Star customer qualities

Now go through and prioritize your 5 Star customer qualities in order of importance, making sure that the non-negotiable quality remains at the top of your list.

My 5 Star customer qualities

1. _____

2. _____

3. _____

4. _____

5. _____

When prioritizing, consider which quality is most important and why.

Step 5: Test your 5 Star customer qualities

Now you have identified your 5 Star customer qualities, you need to test them by checking that they relate to your existing customers. The objective is to check that your top five customer qualities are accurate and easily verifiable.

This is where you could find that you do not know as much about your customers as you would like and there may be a need to do some research. Alternatively, you may discover that you need to do some fine-tuning and refine your list of 5 Star qualities.

In a spreadsheet, get a list of your customers and score each one based on the number of qualities they have. Customers get one point for each of the 5 Star qualities they have.

Customers with all five of these qualities, therefore, will have a score of 5 and customers with just two qualities will have a score of 2.

If you are unable to tell whethr they have one or more of the qualities, it might suggest that you need to make your qualities more tangible. You should also review your qualities if all your customers have fewer than 3 stars or if all your customers have scores of 5.

It is worth getting this right as it will become the foundation of our lead generation activities. The more specific we are, the easier the lead generation will become. The chances are that you will still attract a wider audience and as long as they have the non-negotiable quality then you will still do business with them. However, if you are going to get new customers, why not get 5 Star customers?

NEXT STEPS

Now you know what an ideal customer looks like, the next step is to begin to understand why they may be interested in buying your products and services.

👍 TAKEAWAYS

What have I learned?

1. What is the difference between a sales lead and a sales opportunity?

_____

_____

_____

_____

_____

_____

_____

_____

2. Why is it important to take a targeted approach to sales lead generation?

_____

_____

_____

_____

_____

_____

_____

_____

3. Why is it important to profile your ideal customers?

_____

_____

_____

_____

_____

_____

_____

_____

_____

_____

_____

_____

_____

_____

_____

_____

_____

_____

_____

_____

_____

_____

2 FINDING THE PAIN

✔ OUTCOMES FROM THIS CHAPTER

- Understand your ideal customers' buying motives
- Understand how pain drives business-to-business sales
- Discover your customers' various buying motives

COACHING SESSION 5

Self-assessment

Assessment criteria	Score
I understand why my ideal customers buy my products and services.	
I understand the difference between problems and pain.	
I am aware of the relevant problems my ideal customers face.	
I focus on one or two buying motives which best suit my products and services.	
I use these buying motives to direct my lead generation actives.	
TOTAL	

Score yourself between 1 and 5. A score of 5 means this statement is totally true; 1 means this statement is totally untrue. Total up your score. The maximum is 25 out of 25. Even if you give yourself a full score, I recommend you complete this chapter.

EMOTION DRIVES BUYING BEHAVIOUR

If we want to attract ideal customers, we need to understand what is motivating their buying behaviour. This is so that we can tailor our sales messages to appeal to their buying motives. It is their buying motives that will determine what form of words we need to use to gain their attention and generate their interest in having a sales conversation about our products and services.

Your ideal customers may or may not be in the market looking to buy the specific products and services you provide. However, at any one time, many will have problems that your products and services can fix. Taking a problem-based approach to sales lead generation will increase the number of people who become interested in having a sales conversation, especially if your ideal customers do not realize they need your products and services or why they should buy from you rather than one of your competitors.

Many people involved in sales refer to 'customer pain' when they are actually talking about problems that a customer has. We all have problems to deal with in life. However, we are totally unaware of many of our problems. Even if we are aware of those problems, we may not be prepared to spend money to resolve them. It is only when a problem becomes painful that we become motivated to do something about it. The stronger the emotion, the more buying motivation your potential customers will have and the more willing they will be to have a sales conversation with anyone who can help them resolve their buying motivation. Here are some examples of how emotion can drive buying behaviour:

- Anger at being let down by a supplier
- Worry about missing an important deadline
- Frustration that sales are not growing fast enough
- Anxiety about being fined for non-compliance

The bottom line is that unless our ideal customers are dissatisfied with the current or future status quo then they are unlikely to have a motivation to change from the status quo. Even if we got them interested in having a sales conversation, we will probably be wasting our time if they do not have a compelling reason to change from the status quo.

In sales, the best way to think of emotion is 'the motive for action' and if that motive is strong enough then we know they will be looking to do something about it. At this point they will be open to change from the status quo and open to suggestions for how to resolve the pain.

When seeking to generate interest, if we focus too much on specific products we lose relevance to our target audience and their problems. The classic marketing line is:

'People do not buy a drill, they buy a hole.'

The buyer wants to drill a hole in a wall and the problem is that they do not have the right tools to do the job. They have a hole-drilling problem. What is more interesting is why being able to drill a hole is important to them. The chances are that there could be a number of variations on the hole-drilling problem. For example:

- They are not very good at DIY.
- Their existing drill has stopped working.

- Their existing drill is not the right type.
- The hole is an unusual size.
- The surface they are drilling into is unstable.

We need to recognize that our ideal customers may have many different reasons why they might be interested in talking to us about our products and services. However, there will always be one motive that is stronger than the rest: their primary motive.

COACHING SESSION 6

Fill in the missing blanks. See the end of the chapter for the answers.

People are not interested in our products and services; they are interested in solving their

_____. Without the _____ to buy there will not be a sale. The bigger the

_____ the greater the _____ to change from the _____.

VALUE PROPOSITIONS

From a lead generation point of view, I would like you to start thinking in terms of value propositions rather than products and services. In the example above, where I was referring to the difference between a customer wanting a hole rather than a drill, the drill is the product and the hole is the value proposition. In other words, if you buy my drill you will get a hole. Different drill suppliers would then have variations on the value proposition. For example:

Problem	Value proposition
They are not very good at DIY.	Easy to use
Their existing drill has stopped working.	Reliability
Their existing drill is not the right type.	Versatility
The hole is an unusual size.	Versatility
The surface they are drilling into is unstable.	Versatility

If your target audience is people who are not very good at DIY then you may focus your messaging around the value proposition of ease of use, even though your drills may also be reliable and versatile.

The other reason for talking about propositions rather than products and services is that you may have a number of potential ways of delivering value, which can involve one or more of your products and services.

Example

dmClub is a business providing telephony-related products and services to small businesses. They have many products and services but three main propositions:

Value proposition	Related products and services
Handling incoming business calls	dmConnect, dmConnect12, dmSwitchboard12, dmVoice, ProVoiceover, ProTime, Gold Numbers
Answering business calls on your behalf	dmAnswers, dmVoice, Voicemail
Receiving faxes via email	dmFax

You will notice that some products and services will be relevant to more than one value proposition. Your product is the vehicle for delivering value to your ideal customers and the value comes from helping your customer resolve a specific problem that is motivating their buying behaviour.

The way it works is that we focus our communication on our value proposition that generates interest. Then we use the consultative sales process to establish what products and services the customer needs. If customers come to us asking about specific products and services, we take a step back and find out what is motivating their buying behaviour and take the conversation up to the value proposition level.

Even though a potential customer may sound as if they know what they want, we should still check, so that we can discover what will help us win the sale and also to make sure the customer gets the right solution for their needs.

We will be covering the consultative sale process in depth in Part 2 of this book. In the rest of Part 1 we will be working on your proposition. If you have only one product, then assume that your product is the proposition.

COACHING SESSION 7

Have a go at identifying your value propositions. Some businesses just have one but many have more than one.

Value proposition	Related products and services

CUSTOMER ARCHETYPES

A simple way I have developed for quickly understanding buying motivation is called 'customer archetypes'. The objective is to identify the different buying motives our target audience may have for a specific value proposition. We can then look at which of our customers fitted that archetype when they first purchased that proposition so that we can start to build a picture and gain insights which will help us when we get to crafting our sales messages.

We will do this in four steps:

Step 1 – Identify the problems

Step 2 – Create your customer archetypes

Step 3 – Validate your customer archetypes

Step 4 – Prioritize your customer archetypes

Step 1: Identify the problems

To understand our ideal customers' buying motives, we first need to understand some of the problems they have and how solving those problems will be of benefit.

To begin I would like you to list as many relevant problems your prospects may have.

Example

As an example, I am going to be focusing on dmClub's call-answering value proposition and the problems customers have in relation to call answering.

Problem	Why is it a problem?	How would they benefit from solving the problem?
They currently use a professional call-answering service but can no longer afford it.	Costs too much	Save money
They are too busy to answer all of their incoming calls.	Calls are going unanswered and they could be missing out on sales opportunities.	Increase sales
They want a professional call-answering service but they only have small call volumes.	They cannot find a call-answering service that caters for low call volumes.	Increase sales
They are not responding quickly enough to important customers.	Risk of losing business	Keep existing customers

Problem	Why is it a problem?	How would they benefit from solving the problem?
They are not happy with the service levels of their existing call-answering solution.	Risk of losing business	Keep existing customers
They cannot find a professional call-answering service they can afford.	Could be missing out on sales opportunities	Increase sales
They are getting too many cold calls.	Wasting too much time	Increase productivity
They have times when they need extra help answering the phones, e.g. lunch-time.	It is difficult to find quality resources that can be available at short notice.	Increase sales Keep existing customers

COACHING SESSION 8

Select one of your value propositions and complete this exercise.

Problem	Why is it a problem?	How would they benefit from solving the problem?

Step 2: Create your customer archetypes

Now we have a better sense of the relevant problems that your ideal customers are facing, we can start to look at why they might be interested in having a sales conversation.

We will come up with five or six primary motives and give them names that we can use as shorthand. The names are important as they should give us a clue as to the motivation. Using these names makes them easier to remember and to distinguish.

Remember that a prospect may have several buying motives and with customer archetypes we are looking for the one that is most important to them.

Example

Here are the customer archetypes for dmClub's call-answering proposition:

Archetype	Buying motivation
The Sellers	They are worried that they are missing sales-related calls.
The Improvers	They are dissatisfied with the quality of their existing professional call-answering service.
The Occasionals	They need help with call answering but not very often and unpredictably. They are frustrated at having to pay for a monthly contract for a service they rarely use.
The Cost Cutters	They already have a professional call-answering service but are eager to save money.
The Time Savers	They are frustrated at the amount of time they spend on non-important calls.
The Budgeters	They sometimes need extra call-answering capacity but they are worried about committing to a monthly contract for a service they rarely use.

COACHING SESSION 9

Now identify your customer archetypes for your proposition.

Archetype	Buying motivation

Step 3: Validate your customer archetypes

Now that you have your customer archetypes, I recommend that you validate them against your existing customer list. More specifically, identify the customers who have previously purchased a product or service related to the proposition that we are working on.

You are looking for their buying motivation for initially being interested in having a sales conversation. This information will help you attract more of the same.

You may need to skip this step if you do not yet have any paying customers for your proposition.

COACHING SESSION 10

For each of your customer archetypes, give one or more examples of an existing customer who had that primary buying motivation when they first started talking to you about a particular proposition.

Archetype	Examples

Step 4: Prioritize your customer archetypes

I recommend that you do not try to cover all the customer archetypes and instead focus on the top three buying motives that are strongest with your ideal customers.

Example

Priority	Archetype	Reason for priority
1	The Sellers	The sales motive will make the sale easier for smaller businesses to justify the cost.
2	The Budgeters	dmAnswers14 is a flexible and affordable service with several unique features that enable customers to minimize costs without compromising on call-answering quality.
3	The Occasionals	dmAnswers14 is available on a pay-as-you go basis and is perfect for customers with low and/or irregular call volumes.

You will see that the selection criteria used above have started to allude to product features, but in another business we could equally have been considering products or services included in that proposition. We will be looking at features in the next chapter. For now, we are just looking at which archetypes are likely to work best for us. In the above example, there is also a potential synergy between the three archetypes. You could easily have prospects with a limited budget and irregular call volumes that want to ensure that they capture sales-related calls. It's not a problem if your top three do not have such a synergy.

COACHING SESSION 11

Now prioritize your top three customer archetypes.

Priority	Archetype	Reason for priority
1		

2		
3		

ONLINE RESOURCE

Customer archetypes

You can download copies of all these 'customer archetypes' sheets from:

www.TYCoachbooks.com/Sales

ANSWERS TO COACHING SESSION 6

People are not interested in our products and services; they are interested in solving their **problems**.

Without the **motivation** to buy there will not be a sale. The bigger the **pain** the greater the **motivation** to change from the **status quo**.

NEXT STEPS

So far we have clarified *who* your ideal customers are and *why* they may be interested in speaking to you about one of your propositions. There are probably many aspects of your products and services you can talk about. The trick is to match what you emphasize with the main buying motives of your ideal customers. The next step, therefore, is to clarify *what* aspects of our proposition we should emphasize so that we can appear different from our competition and stand out from the crowd.

TAKEAWAYS

What have I learned?

1. What is buying motivation?

_____

_____

_____

_____

_____

_____

_____

_____

_____

_____

_____

_____

2. Why is it important to understand the buying motives of your ideal customers?

_____

_____

_____

_____

_____

_____

_____

_____

_____

_____

_____

_____

3. What is the difference between problems and pain and why does it matter?

_____

_____

_____

_____

_____

_____

_____

_____

_____

_____

_____

_____

_____

_____

_____

_____

_____

_____

_____

_____

_____

_____

_____

_____

3 | YOUR USP

 OUTCOMES FROM THIS CHAPTER

- Understand the importance of having a USP
- Know the difference between features and benefits
- Find your USP

COACHING SESSION 12

Self-assessment

Assessment criteria	Score
I have a USP for the product, service or proposition I am generating leads for.	
I understand the difference between features and benefits.	
For the product, service or proposition I am generating leads for, I have a list of relevant features and benefits.	
For the product, service or proposition I am generating leads for, I know how the features compare to those of my main competitors.	
For the product, service or proposition I am generating leads for, I know which aspects to emphasize to attract my ideal customers.	
TOTAL	

Score yourself between 1 and 5. A score of 5 means this statement is totally true; 1 means this statement is totally untrue. Total up your score. The maximum is 25 out of 25. Even if you give yourself a full score, I recommend you complete this chapter.

YOUR UNIQUE SELLING PROPOSITION

When we start talking about our products and services, we need to find something different to say compared to our competitors. We need a unique selling proposition, more commonly known as a USP. This is because the human brain is wired to notice things that are different. When everything is the same, our brains tend to zone out, as we would when listening to someone with a monotone voice or staring at a brick wall!

If we are communicating similar messages in a similar place to everyone else, then we are unlikely to be noticed. The other reason for having a USP is that, should we be noticed by potential customers, having something unique will make it easier to justify having higher prices than our competitors. However, it is not enough to show that we are different from our competitors. The difference needs to be relevant to the buying motives of our ideal customers.

FEATURES ARE NOT ATTRACTIVE

In order to attract the attention of potential customers, we need to find an aspect of our proposition that is not only different but also appealing. A common problem is that we get too close to our products and services and what we think is special about our products and services is of little interest to potential customers. Finding the angle is about homing in on the aspects of our products and services that will resonate with our potential customers' primary buying motives.

Features are important in telling your prospective customers what they get for their money. At some point in their buying process, when they are researching their options, they will be assessing and comparing features. However, to generate that all-important initial interest, we need to appeal to their primary buying motivation.

For the remainder of this chapter I am going to help you find the unique aspects of your proposition that we will emphasize when we start to look at your messaging. This will be happen in five simple steps.

Step 1 – List the features

What I would like you to do to begin with is simply to list out the main features of your product, service, or proposition. We will then take this list and use it to unlock the real value that your ideal customers will find attractive.

Example

Here is a list of features of dmClub's call-answering service that we have been highlighting in previous chapters.

Feature	Description
Front Desk	We answer your calls for you in your company name and according to your instructions.
Message Desk	We answer calls in your company name and take a message when you miss a call.
24/7	The service is available 24 hours a day, 7 days per week.
Smartphone console	Enables you to instantly change how we handle your calls.
Direct Mode	Enables you to switch off Front Desk so that you can answer calls directly.
Geographic telephone number	You get to choose a geographical phone number for anywhere in the UK.
Flexible setup	Calls can be answered for your whole company, a specific team, or just specific individuals.
PAYG	The service is available on a pay-as-you-go basis with no minimum monthly commitment.
UK-based agents	All of our agents are UK based and professionally trained.

COACHING SESSION 13

Now list the main features of your product, service, or proposition.

Feature	Description

Step 2 – Identify differences

We are now ready to start analysing our feature list and comparing it to our competitors'. As you begin to do this exercise and start looking a little more closely at your competitors, you may find that you need to revise your feature list. Maybe you will need to add in a feature that has been overlooked. Alternatively, you may need to rename a feature that is very different but does not appear to be different.

We are going to simply go through your feature list and score each feature based on how different it is from your competitors'. Simply score the differences as high, medium, or low. As you go through the exercise, it is important that you are as objective as possible.

Example: dmAnswers14 – Professional call-answering service

Feature	Difference	How is the feature different?
Front Desk	Low	N/A
Message Desk	Low	N/A
24/7	Low	N/A
Smartphone console	Medium	N/A
Direct Mode	High	Enables you to turn the service on and off to suit your needs.
Call-answering software	High	You get a virtual business line integrated with dmAnswers14.
Flexible setup	High	You can choose what type of calls you apply the service to, e.g. only sales-related calls.
PAYG	Medium	N/A
UK-based agents	Low	N/A

There are a few observations to make about the above example. The biggest one is that the main features that most people would associate with professional call answering are not that different. While professional call answering on a pay-as-you-go basis is currently quite rare in the UK, it is not unique and it was classified as medium because other features have bigger differences.

COACHING SESSION 14

Now do the exercise on your proposition.

Feature	Difference	How is the feature different?

Step 3 – Identify relevance

Having a feature that is different does not make your proposition attractive to your ideal customers until you relate it to their buying motives. When you start to indicate that your proposition can enable ideal customers to solve their problems, then it starts to become very attractive to them.

We therefore need to look at how relevant our features are to the specific buying motives of our ideal customers. We will be looking out for features that are both different and relevant.

Example 1: dmAnswers14 – Customer archetype: Sellers

Feature	Difference	Relevance	How does the feature help?
Front Desk	Low	High	You will not miss sales-related calls.
Message Desk	Low	High	You will not miss sales-related calls.
24/7	Low	Medium	Ensures you capture out-of-hours sales enquiries.
Smartphone console	Medium	Low	Quickly change how we answer calls for you.
Direct Mode	High	High	You only need use the service when you are unable to answer calls yourself.
Call-handling software	High	High	You can receive sales calls directly, even if you are out of the office.
Flexible setup	High	High	You can use the service just for sales-related calls.
PAYG	Medium	Medium	You only pay when we answer a call for you.
UK-based agents	Low	Medium	Your prospects will get a good first impression.

Example 2: dmAnswers14 – Customer archetype: Budgeters

Feature	Difference	Relevance	How does the feature help?
Front Desk	Low	Medium	You can limit this service to specific types of call.
Message Desk	Low	Medium	You can limit this service to specific types of call and use voicemail for anyone else.
24/7	Low	Low	This is optional.
Smartphone console	Medium	Medium	You can save money by varying the way we answer calls for you.
Direct Mode	High	High	You can decide when you answer your own calls and when we answer them for you.
Call-handling software	High	High	Eliminate many of the hidden costs of professional call answering.
Flexible setup	High	High	You can save money by using the service for specific types of call.
PAYG	Medium	High	There are no commitments for minimum usage. Packages are available once you know your regular call volumes.
UK-based agents	Low	Medium	You do not need to sacrifice quality to save money.

Example 3: dmAnswers14 – Customer archetype: Occasionals

Feature	Difference	Relevance	How does the feature help?
Front Desk	Low	Low	You can turn the service on and off. You only pay for the calls we answer.
Message Desk	Low	Low	You can turn the service on and off. You only pay for the calls we answer.
24/7	Low	Low	You can turn the service on and off. You only pay for the calls we answer.
Smartphone console	Medium	High	You can quickly change when and how we handle calls for you.
Direct Mode	High	High	You can turn the service on and off to suit your needs.
Call-handling software	High	High	Our special call-handling software enables us to provide the UK's most flexible professional call-answering service.
Flexible setup	High	High	We can answer calls for the whole company, for certain types of call, and for specific individuals.
PAYG	Medium	High	There are no minimum monthly commitments. Just use the service when you need it.
UK-based agents	Low	Medium	All of our agents are UK based and professionally trained.

⛉⛉ COACHING SESSION 15

Customer archetype 1

Do the exercise on your highest-priority customer archetype.

Feature	Difference	Relevance	How does the feature help?

Customer archetype 2

Do the exercise on your second-highest-priority customer archetype.

Feature	Difference	Relevance	How does the feature help?

Customer archetype 3

Do the exercise on your third-highest-priority customer archetype.

Feature	Difference	Relevance	How does the feature help?

Step 4 – Prioritize and refine

Our customers and prospects will be most likely to be attracted by the features that are both different and enable them to solve their problem. We now need to prioritize the features in order of how they benefit the customer archetype. We will also refine the wording so that it becomes more specific. You will notice, in the examples below, that the further down the feature list we go, the more generic the statements are. Features that are highly relevant and different are much more specific.

Example: dmAnswers14 – Customer archetype: Sellers

Feature	Difference	Relevance	How does the feature help?
Flexible Setup	High	High	You only need use the service for sales-related calls.
Direct Mode	High	High	You can turn the service on and off to suit your needs.
Call-handling software	High	High	You can receive sales calls directly, even if you are out of the office.
Front Desk	Low	High	When you are busy and unavailable we answer sales-related calls for you in your company name and according to your instructions.

Message Desk	Low	High	If you get a sales-related call when you are on the other line or away from your desk, we answer the call in your company name and take a message according to your instructions.
24/7	Low	Medium	The service is available 24 hours a day, 7 days a week.
UK-based agents	Low	Medium	All of our agents are UK based and professionally trained.
PAYG	Medium	Medium	The service is available on a pay-as-you-go basis.
Smartphone console	Medium	Low	You have full control over how we answer calls for you and changes are instantly updated.

You will notice that, while cost is an issue for both the Budgeter and Occasional customer archetypes, it is not something we need to emphasize for Sellers. We keep the focus on how the service will help ideal customers avoid missing sales calls. Cost may be an issue for Sellers but it is not the main reason why they are looking for professional call answering. They will be thinking about the cost of missing a sales opportunity.

The focus of the Sellers, motivation is on sales-related calls and the prospect of being able to limit the call-answering service to sales-related calls is something that could be very appealing. Therefore it makes sense to emphasize this aspect of dmAnswers14 in any lead generation activity focused on attracting Seller archetypes. When seeking to attract Budgeter or Occasional customer archetypes, however, the prioritization of the features and benefits to focus on will be totally different.

COACHING SESSION 16

Complete the tables by putting the features in order of priority and refining the wording to make it more specific.

Customer archetype 1

Feature	Difference	Relevance	How does the feature help?

Customer archetype 2

Feature	Difference	Relevance	How does the feature help?

Customer archetype 3

Feature	Difference	Relevance	How does the feature help?

Step 5 – Look for common themes

Now that you have done the exercise for your three top archetypes, you should start to get some common themes among the key areas of attraction. The ideal situation is that we are able to create some common themes so that we can create messaging that can be shared for our top three customer archetypes. It is not always possible but it is worth trying because it will mean less work when we get to crafting our messages. Rather than having three totally separate pitches for each customer archetype, it is better to have one central theme and just vary part of the message depending on whom we are talking to.

Example – dmAnswers14

COMMON THEMES

1. Common themes are the desire for quality professional call answering on a flexibile and affordable basis.

2. Affordability is a central theme. However, the flexibility of dmAnswers14 is a much stronger theme and it is the flexibility that is the unique selling proposition and something that should be emphasized in any sales and marketing communication.

3. The flexibility enables the Sellers to just use the service for sales-related calls and, even then, only when they are unable to answer calls for themselves.

4. The flexibility allows the Budgeters to get a quality service they can afford, even if they have very low call volumes. They can limit the cost by choosing which types of calls are professionally answered and when they use the service.

5. The flexibility means that the Occasionals can get the quality professional call answering they need at a price they can afford without having to commit to monthly call volumes.

COACHING SESSION 17

Now identify some common themes relative to your proposition's uniqueness and your three top buying motives.

Common themes

1. _____
   _____
   _____
   _____

2. _____
   _____
   _____
   _____

3. _____
   _____
   _____
   _____

4. _____
   _____
   _____
   _____

ONLINE RESOURCE

USP sheets

You can download copies of all the sheets in this chapter from:

www.TYCoachbooks.com/Sales

NEXT STEPS

Now that we understand the buying motives of our target audience and our USP, we are ready to start constructing our sales messages that will generate interest from our ideal customers.

TAKEAWAYS

What have I learned?

1. What is a USP and why is it important to have one?

_____

_____

_____

_____

_____

_____

_____

_____

_____

_____

_____

2. What is the difference between a feature and a benefit?

_____

_____

_____

_____

_____

_____

_____

_____

_____

_____

_____

_____

3. How do we decide which aspects of our product, service or proposition to emphasize?

4

CRAFTING YOUR MESSAGES

 OUTCOMES FROM THIS CHAPTER

- Create a messaging framework
- Understand the purpose of a pitch
- Use your messaging framework to pitch your products and services

COACHING SESSION 18

Self-assessment

Assessment criteria	Score
For any product, service or proposition I am seeking leads for, I have a written pitch.	
I regularly work on my messaging and refine my pitch.	
I have different versions of my pitch for different audiences.	
I have different lengths of pitch for different occasions.	
I have both a 15-second and a 60-second pitch rehearsed so that I can deliver it whenever called upon.	
TOTAL	

Score yourself between 1 and 5. A score of 5 means this statement is totally true; 1 means this statement is totally untrue. Total up your score. The maximum is 25 out of 25. Even if you give yourself a full score, I recommend you complete this chapter.

THE PHRASE THAT PAYS

In sales, words are the tools of the trade. We want our target audience to respond to our words and so we need to invest some time in crafting words that our ideal customers want to hear. Your pitch is the vehicle for delivering your messages and the ideal is to come up with some simple phraseology that encapsulates your message succinctly and in a way that potential customers find attractive. In short, it pays to work on our sales messages so that they have maximum impact on our ideal customers.

THE POWER OF SCRIPTS

Think about your favourite movie. The actors in that movie would all have had lines taken from the movie script. The actors learn their lines and when the movie is made they can be more spontaneous because they have learned their lines. The same is true with sales. All of the top salespeople I know work from scripts. They work on what they will say in advance and take time to craft their sales messages so that it sounds as if it is the first time they have uttered those words. Yet their words will be 100 per cent consistent 100 per cent of the time.

I recommend you script out what you plan to say, learn the script, practise it and then throw the script away! Your messaging will evolve and get even better results over time. There should be a central theme to the messages you use in your scripts and this comes from your messaging framework.

MESSAGING FRAMEWORK

Up to this point in the book, we have been working towards a messaging framework. A messaging framework is simply a co-ordinated collection of core messages which we can then use as a reference when we talk about our products and services. We would use this framework in both our sales and marketing activities. The more products, services and propositions you have to sell, and the more people that are involved in sales and marketing activities, the more important it is to have a documented messaging framework that everyone can refer to.

There are seven questions we need to answer for our messaging framework:

- What are you selling me?
- How is it different?
- Why should I be interested?
- What can it do for me?
- What results can I expect?
- Why should I believe you?
- How do I find out more?

As we are crafting our messages, we need to aim for something that is simple and easy to understand for anyone listening to the message. There is a limit to the amount of information that most people can absorb and remember and we need to continually strive for simple messages that are attractive to our ideal customers. Remember, it is the relevance to our ideal customers' buying motives that makes our sales messages attractive to them.

Example – dmAnswers14

Question	Response
What are you selling me?	We provide a flexible professional call-answering service that is affordable for any size of business.
How is it different?	The service is so flexible that you can restrict the service to certain types of call such as sales enquiries.
Why should I be interested?	You should be interested if:
Reason 1	You want to avoid missing sales enquiries when you are busy or unavailable.
Reason 2	You have a limited budget for professional call-answering but you do not want to compromise on quality.
Reason 3	You only need a professionally call-answering service when you are short-staffed or for special occasions.
What results can I expect?	You will save money without compromising on quality because you can limit the service to where in the business you need it most.
Why should I believe you?	We have been providing innovative telephony solutions to small businesses for over 22 years. We also provide a 14-day money-back guarantee if you are not completely satisfied.
How do I find out more?	Contact us today and we will show you how you can get quality professional call answering for your business at a price you can afford.

COACHING SESSION 19

Now complete the answers to the following questions for your product, service or proposition.

Question	Response
What are you selling me?	
How is it different?	
Why should I be interested?	You should be interested if:

Reason 1	
Reason 2	
Reason 3	
What results can I expect?	
Why should I believe you?	
How do I find out more?	

THE 15-SECOND PITCH

There are times when you want the answer to a simple question like 'What do you do?' and you should be able to respond with something simple that has a hook in it so that it causes the other person to ask more.

In 15 seconds you have time to say around 35 words, which should be enough to join together the first two messages from the messaging framework:

'What are you selling me?' and 'How are you different?'

If the two sentences do not flow or the combined length is much longer than 35 words, you may want to go back and refine your messaging framework.

You can use this 15-second pitch for casual conversations when you meet new people and they ask you what you do. You can also use it as a key element of your introduction when networking or cold calling.

Example – dmAnswers14

THE 15-SECOND PITCH

'We provide a flexible professional call-answering service that is affordable for any size of business. The service is so flexible that you can restrict the service to certain types of call such as sales enquiries.'

COACHING SESSION 20

Now put together your 15-second pitch In two sentences.

_____

_____

_____

_____

_____

_____

_____

THE 60-SECOND PITCH

With longer pitches you have more time to build the interest and your pitch should have certain key elements:

- Your proposition
- Your credibility
- The problem
- The solution
- Your call to action

The above is based on a 60-second pitch at a business networking meeting. Sixty seconds equates to around ten words for your name and the name of your company plus 140 words to get the essence of your message across.

Example – dmAnswers14

Element	Message
Your proposition	We provide a flexible professional call-answering service that's affordable for any size of business.
Your credibility	We've been providing innovative telephony solutions to small businesses for over 22 years.
The problem	If a potential customer calls when you are busy or unavailable, that sales opportunity could be lost for ever. However, using a professional call-answering service can get very expensive, especially if you do not get many calls or you only need the service occasionally when you are short-staffed.
The solution	dmAnswers14 is the UK's most flexible professional call-answering service that is affordable for any size of business. It is available on a pay-as-you-go basis and so flexible that you can turn the service on and off to suit your needs and you can even restrict the service to specific types of call.
Call to action	If you're looking for flexible and affordable professional call answering, then please give me a call.

COACHING SESSION 21

Now put together your 60-second pitch.

Element	Message
Your proposition	
Your credibility	
The problem	
Your solution	
Call to action	

SOFT PITCHING

There are many times when you want to generate interest but a pitch is not appropriate – for example, when you are at a social gathering or talking to an existing customer. Imagine you are talking to your most important customer and you don't want to sound as if you are selling and risk damaging your trusted relationship. The problem with pitches is that if we sound too 'salesy' then we risk losing trust. This is a big problem if we want to be seen as a trusted adviser. Soft pitching provides a gentle and effective way of generating interest conversationally without seeming to be selling.

Soft pitching involves telling a story that communicates the value of your solution. You give an example of how a customer with a similar problem has benefited from your proposition. However, rather than just telling the story once your customer has mentioned the problem, you can tell the story to see if the customer has the problem. The stories, if crafted properly, should blend into normal conversation.

A soft pitch has the following components:

- A customer suffering from the problem
- The results from working with you
- A short sentence linking the two together

The problem

This part of the story is the most important and should be about 60 per cent of the content. It should be about a specific person who is suffering from one of your three main problems that feature in your messaging framework. We want similar people with similar problems to relate to the story. You will get one of three responses from the person you are speaking with:

- They say out loud or to themselves, 'That's just like me.'
- They say out loud or to themselves, 'I know someone like that.'
- They offer no response and you just continue your conversation.

You should be clear about the distinction between customers and consumers. Customers are the people who *pay* for the product or service. A consumer is someone who uses the product or service. In many cases they may be the same, but when they are different then the person in the story should be the person you are looking to influence, which would normally be the customer.

Here is one example of how to state a problem:

'One of our customers is a business owner who contacted us because he was trying to take his first holiday in five years. He had not taken a holiday previously because he was too worried that a potential customer would call while he was away and he would miss out on the business. He had heard about professional call-answering and was looking for his phones to be answered for a week and to only be contacted if a sales call came through. He was getting frustrated because he could not find a professional call-answering company prepared to do just one week. They all wanted to sign him up for a three-month contract.'

The results

'Anyway, he got away on holiday and was able to relax, knowing that if a sales opportunity did come through he would hear about it.'

The link

This is a very short sentence to link the problem with the results. Its only real purpose is to link the two together and make the story flow. Here are some typical examples:

- 'I was referred to the customer.'

- 'I was asked to look at the problem.'

- 'A friend recommended dmAnswers14 – she is a customer who uses the service every now and then when she is short-staffed.'

CRAFTING YOUR SOFT PITCH

Like a 60-second pitch, the story should be capable of being told in 140 words. You keep it short by not talking about how you solved their problem.

When you bring it together, it should total about 140 words so that you can introduce yourself and tell your story in under a minute. There will normally be some refining to do to make it flow and to keep it short. Normally, that involves removing unnecessary verbiage which is not essential to the message. Often, these extra words are trying to add unnecessary detail or trying to sell.

'One of our customers is a business owner who contacted us because he was trying to take his first holiday in five years. He was worried that he would miss a sales enquiry while he was away and had called a few professional call-answering companies but was getting incredibly frustrated because he only wanted the service for a week and they all wanted to sign him up for a three-month contract!

'A friend recommended dmAnswers14 – she is a customer who uses the service every now and then when she is short-staffed.

'Anyway, he got away on holiday and was able to relax, knowing that if a sales opportunity did come through he would hear about it.'

COACHING SESSION 22

Now create a soft pitch for your product, service or proposition.

Section	Narrative
Problem	
Link	
Results	

HOW TO USE YOUR SOFT PITCH

Social gatherings

Your soft pitch is designed to slip into normal day-to-day conversation. For example, if you meet someone in a social setting such as a sports club or at a party and they ask you what you do, you can use a variation of your 15-second pitch and then use your soft pitch as an illustration:

'I work for a telephony company that provides a flexible professional call-answering service that is affordable for any size of business. The service is so flexible that you can restrict the service to certain types of call such as sales enquiries.

'For example, one of our customers is a business owner ...'

Networking

In a similar way to social gatherings, soft pitching is ideal for informal networking where people ask you what you do. It can also be used as an effective alternative to a 60-second pitch at the type of networking gatherings that get everyone to introduce themselves. The story will always be more memorable than a regular pitch and is more likely to connect with people in the room who have the same problem or know someone who does. The ideal scenario is having 30 people all telling your story to people they know!

Talking to customers

Whenever your customer asks you how you are and what you have been doing lately, it is a cue to launch into an appropriate soft pitch. You can have many different stories which all follow a similar structure. The trick is to weave them into general conversation so that they just sound like a regular anecdote.

ONLINE RESOURCE

Messaging framework

You can download copies of the sheets used in this chapter from:

www.TYCoachbooks.com/Sales

NEXT STEPS

Now that we have developed our sales messages so that they are focused on the problems our target audience have that we can solve, and emphasize why they should want to talk to us, it is time to start communicating our messages to our target audience.

TAKEAWAYS

What have I learned?

1. What is a messaging framework?

_____

_____

_____

_____

_____

_____

_____

_____

_____

2. Why is it important to have a messaging framework?

_____

_____

_____

_____

_____

_____

_____

_____

_____

3. What is the difference between a regular pitch and a soft pitch?

GENERATING INTEREST

 OUTCOMES FROM THIS CHAPTER

- Calculate how many leads you need to generate
- Know how to approach lead generation
- Have six alternatives to cold calling

COACHING SESSION 23

Self-assessment

Assessment criteria	Score
I know how many more sales leads I need to generate each month.	
I routinely scheduled account reviews with customers.	
I routinely ask customers for referrals and seek cross-selling and up-selling opportunities.	
I have a network of introducers who pass me sales leads.	
I use every opportunity to expand my network of contacts.	
TOTAL	

Score yourself between 1 and 5. A score of 5 means this statement is totally true; 1 means this statement is totally untrue. Total up your score. The maximum is 25 out of 25. Even if you give yourself a full score, I recommend you complete this chapter.

HOW MANY SALES LEADS DO YOU NEED?

Before we spend time going through specific sources of sales lead, we should work out how many sales leads you currently require. To do this, we need to look at some key aspects of your sales:

- Your monthly target
- Your average sales value
- Your sales conversion rate

Monthly target

If you do not have a monthly sales target then it is worth setting yourself one. Decide how much you need to sell in a year to produce the income you require and then use that to work out a monthly sales target.

Average sales value

This is how much, on average, each sale is worth. This will enable you to work out how many sales you need to make each month, For example, if your monthly target is £50,000 and your average sales value is £5,000, then you know you need to make, on average, ten sales per month to reach your target.

Sales conversion rate

Your sales conversion rate represents how many sales leads you currently require, on average, to win a sale. For example, if you need five sales leads to win one sale then your sales conversion rate is 20 per cent. Improving your sales conversion rate will reduce the number of sales leads you require and we will be working on that in Part 2 of this book. For now we should work from your existing sales conversion rate.

Once you have these three numbers, then you can compare it with your average monthly sales to work out how many extra sales leads you require.

Example

My monthly sales target	£50,000
My average monthly sales	£30,000
Shortfall	£20,000
My average sales value	£5,000
Extra sales required to reach my target	4
My sales conversion rate	25%
Extra sales leads required	16

COACHING SESSION 24

Now set yourself a monthly sales target, calculate your average sales value and sales conversion rate and determine how many sales leads you need per month and your current shortfall.

My monthly sales target	
My average monthly sales	
Shortfall	
My average sales value	
Extra sales required to reach my target	
My sales conversion rate	
Extra sales leads required	

YOU DON'T HAVE TO COLD CALL

International sales trainer Frank Furness says that 'Cold calling is the price you pay for not generating sales leads in other ways' and many salespeople manage to generate more than enough sales leads to meet their requirements without cold calling. In this chapter I am going to cover the six main sources of sales lead which you should be looking at. I would like you not to have to depend on marketing activities to generate the sales leads you require. You need to be able to make up any shortfall with your own lead generation activities.

Lead generation is the thing that most salespeople I have met find the hardest aspect of selling. The sign of a good salesperson is someone who is continually on the lookout for interest. The more sales leads you generate, the easier it becomes to reach your sales targets because you can start to get very fussy about which sales leads you pursue.

The work we have done earlier has been the groundwork for sales lead generation and now is the time to bring it all together and start talking to our target audience. The hard part is getting them to want to talk to you. The way it was explained to me was to imagine you want to feed breadcrumbs to pigeons. They want the breadcrumbs but if we just charge at them they will fly away, thinking we mean them harm. Instead, we should just take the time to earn their trust, scatter some crumbs and wait. The pigeons will start to peck at the crumbs and if we show that we are no danger they will eventually start eating out of our hand.

We have done a lot of work so far to identify what your ideal customers will find attractive based on their problems and buying motives. We need them to hear about what you can do for them but the secret is to do it in an unsalesy way. The bottom line is that if our ideal customers have buying motivation then they will want to do something about it. One way or another, we need them to find out that we can help them solve their problem.

The factor that makes a big difference in winning sales is the existence of a trusted relationship. If we have a trusted relationship with an existing customer then, all other things being equal, they are more likely to buy from us and recommend us to people who trust them. Trust is an incredibly important dynamic in sales. Who are you likely to trust more, someone you don't know who calls you out of the blue about a specific product or someone recommended to you by a trusted friend who is already a happy customer?

COACHING SESSION 25

Before we look at additional sources of sales lead, list your existing sources and how many leads you generate, on average, from each source.

Existing lead generation activity	Average sales leads per month
1.	
2.	
3.	
TOTAL	

Even though some of your existing lead generation activities may not currently be bearing fruit, it may be worth applying what you have learned in previous chapters.

CUSTOMER REFERRALS

A happy customer is often willing to make a recommendation to someone they know who may have a similar problem. Occasionally, customers will make a referral without being prompted but the best way to approach referrals is to make asking for referrals part of your sales process.

When you are selling a solution to a problem then there are two points at which you should ask for a referral: when they have agreed to buy from you; and when the problem is solved or they are happy with the progress. Asking at the point of sale works well if you already have a trusted relationship with the person or if you are selling something simple. Otherwise, the better time to ask is once they have seen the impact. What you can do, however, at the point of sale is to set up the future conversation about referrals.

The important thing is to work out how you will ask for referrals and then to build it into your standard process so it is something you do as a matter of course. As with anything in sales, some will give you a referral and some won't but you will get a lot more if you ask. You may want to take them out for a cup of coffee for some product updates and use the opportunity to ask for a referral. If you find it very awkward, then say your boss or your sales coach told you that you should be asking for more referrals!

If your customer knows someone who may be worth referring to, the easiest way to move forward is to ask your customer to make an email introduction. They send an email copied to both their contact and you, making a brief introduction and recommending that their contact speak to you. You could even offer to draft the email for them.

COACHING SESSION 26

Answer the following questions.

1. Which of your existing customers could you ask for a referral?

   _____

   _____

2. What improvements can you make to your sales approach to make asking for referrals easier?

   _____

   _____

ACCOUNT EXTENSION

Often, customers will need additional help to fully solve their problem over and above what they have purchased from you already:

- They may need more of what you have already sold them.

- They may need to buy other products and services to make more progress.

- They may require additional levels of service.

In classic sales terminology, selling more to solve an existing problem is referred to as up-selling.

My recommendation is to build a formal review with your customer into your way of doing business. Mention the review in your proposal and sales conversations so that it is expected. These reviews can be useful for checking progress, seeing what else they need moving forward, and they are also a great opportunity to ask for referrals and testimonials. I also recommend, in the short term, to start doing reviews with your existing customers.

If you know that an existing customer presents an opportunity to extend their account, do not wait until the next meeting. Arrange a meeting with them to review their progress and construct your soft pitch. Indeed, if you are very short on sales leads, arrange a review meeting anyway! You could always combine it with your meeting to talk about referrals.

🗣🗣 COACHING SESSION 27

Go through your customer list and arrange review meetings with your customers. Consider in advance what additional help and support you can offer. Prioritize customers using the 5 Star system from Chapter 2.

Customer	Up-sell opportunity

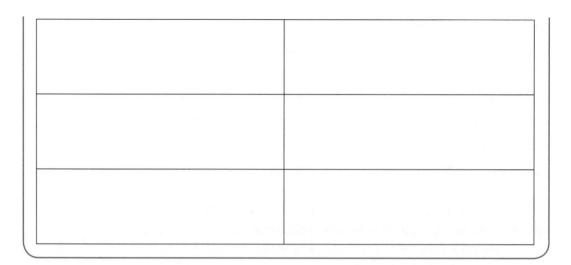

Account expansion

Account expansion is where you are seeking to sell new value propositions to the same customer. In classic sales terminology this would be called cross-selling.

There is often a lot of confusion about the difference between cross-selling and up-selling. The way I differentiate the two is by looking at the value proposition. If you are talking about the same value proposition then it is up-selling – even if you are selling them additional products. If you are talking about a new value proposition then it is cross-selling.

Ideally, your first sale with a customer will be the value proposition where there is the biggest difference from competitors and the most credibility. Once you have made your first sale then it should become easier to cross-sell new value propositions where there is less of a difference from your competitors. One way to generate ideas of cross-selling opportunities is to take the approach used by Amazon: 'People who bought this product also bought that product.' Analyse which value proposition each customer has purchased and see if there are any potential opportunities for cross-selling.

Holding regular account reviews with customers gives you the opportunity to generate interest using the soft pitching approach discussed in the previous chapter.

🗩🗩 COACHING SESSION 28

Create a spreadsheet showing your customer list and which products, services or propositions they have purchased. Look for gaps where one customer has not purchased a product or service that similar customers have. Plan your approach and give them a call to arrange a review.

INTRODUCERS

Introducers, as the name suggests, are people who will introduce you to your ideal customers. The best introducers are the ones who share similar customers to you and who will introduce you to their customer because they believe it is in their customer's best interest rather than because they are getting paid to do so. Introductions can also come from contacts who are not customers but trust the introducer's recommendations. Many introducer relationships work on the basis of reciprocity. If they introduce you to their customers, they will expect the same from you in return.

You should aim to build up a network of introducers who are looking out for opportunities for you. This may take a little time to do but you can speed things up by asking people, including customers who already like and trust you, to connect you to people who may make good introducers. Business networking organizations like BNI are excellent places to find potential introducers and to get introduced to them too. You should check that the organization is focused on referrals rather than people selling to other people in the room.

COACHING SESSION 29

Work out what type of businesses could be a good introducer for you.

Business type	Why they could be a good introducer

Make a list of your best contacts and ask them who they know in those types of businesses. Once they respond, ask them to make an introduction. Draft an email for them to send if you want to ensure that they make the introduction properly.

NETWORKING

Networking is traditionally seen as going to an event and speaking to people at the event in the hope that you may meet potential customers. Business networking events are popular with smaller businesses but there are many other ways to meet people, for example:

- at exhibitions, where your target audience would be attending or displaying
- at conferences on a subject relevant to your proposition
- in special-interest clubs (e.g. golf, gardening, cycling, etc.)
- on public transport (speaking to the person you are sitting next to).

My advice with networking is always to start a conversation in a social context. It could be as simple as asking the other person a question about the event or even making a comment about the weather. When you have a conversation going, ask them what they do. Always do this and only tell them what you do if they ask you back. Then always use an appropriate soft pitch to generate interest.

If you do have hobbies and interests, I recommend joining clubs. The classic example is the golf club, which has traditionally been a place for networking.

COACHING SESSION 30

What networking opportunities could you take advantage of? What groups do you already belong to that you could leverage?

Networking ideas

1.

2.

3.

4.

5.

NEXT STEPS

Now that we have a messaging framework, a pitch and additional sources of sales leads, it is time to start generating more sales leads. In Part 2 of the book I will be helping you win more of your sales opportunities so that, over time, you need fewer sales leads. However, before we do that, we will take a look at the one aspect of sales that many people love to hate – cold calling!

👍 TAKEAWAYS

What have I learned?

1. What is a sales conversion rate and why is it important to sales lead generation?

_____

_____

_____

_____

_____

_____

_____

_____

_____

2. What are account reviews and why are they so important for sales lead generation?

_____

_____

_____

_____

_____

_____

_____

_____

_____

_____

3. What are introducers and how can they help you in your sales?

6 COLD CALLING

✔ OUTCOMES FROM THIS CHAPTER

- Avoid common cold calling mistakes
- Feel more confident about making cold calls
- Introduction and response scripts

🗩🗩 COACHING SESSION 31

Self-assessment

Assessment criteria	Score
I have designed my campaign before calling.	
I always have a compelling business reason for making a call.	
I script my introductions.	
I have scripted answers to each likely response.	
I practise my script before making any important calls.	
TOTAL	

Score yourself between 1 and 5. A score of 5 means this statement is totally true; 1 means this statement is totally untrue. Total up your score. The maximum is 25 out of 25. Even if you give yourself a full score, I recommend you complete this chapter.

MISTAKES PEOPLE MAKE WHEN COLD CALLING

As a source of sales leads, cold calling may not be as effective as customer referrals or personal introductions, but it is an important option, especially if you do not yet have many sales opportunities to work on and while waiting for the strategies outlined in the previous chapter to start bearing fruit. The one good thing about cold calling is that, if you do enough of it, the results are relatively predictable. This means that you can have reasonable certainty that, if you put in a specific amount of effort, over time, then you will get measurable results.

Whether you are considering cold calling or currently making calls and want to feel more confident and get better results, there are some common mistakes you should avoid, as follows.

No compelling business reason

Salespeople and telemarketing companies typically target similar people. The result is that, for decision makers, taking cold calls is considered a huge waste of time. This is because the calls are so often unclear and irrelevant to their top priorities. If they answered every cold call they received, they would never get their day job done. This is why they have gatekeepers to shield them from wasting their time. The trick is to have a reason for calling that is clear and relevant to their job role. If you take a problem-based approach to lead generation and you focus on the problems rather than on your products and services, you are more likely to get some interest. You do need to grab their attention in the first 10 to 15 seconds and so it is important to work on your pitch to make it succinct and relevant.

Sounding like a salesperson

Salespeople tend to sound similar and use the same language, and gatekeepers get wise to the sound of typical salespeople. The default assumption is that a cold caller is a time waster and as soon as one is detected the barriers go up and from then on it is a hard job to convince them otherwise. Some of the most effective cold callers I have met have had a very monotone voice so that they did not sound like a salesperson. They are also careful to avoid specific words such as 'interested' and 'following up' that risk making the barriers come up.

Asking for a face-to-face meeting

The classic desired outcome from a cold call is to seek a meeting with the prospect, which typically lasts an hour. If you assume that everyone, including you, is very busy, then agreeing to an hour is challenging to fit in, especially if the prospect has no idea whether it will be a waste of time or not. If you ask the prospect for an initial ten-minute telephone conversation then you are more likely to get the time and during those ten minutes you can both see whether it would be worth your time and their time to proceed to a full meeting.

Lack of scripting

Many salespeople avoid following scripts because it is obvious when you are reading from a script. As a consequence, they do not have a consistent message and they cannot tell what aspects of their messaging are working. You have a very short space of time to get your message across and it pays to think about it in advance and to practise. Scripts enable you to do this. The trick is to memorize them rather than read them. You should have a collection of vignettes covering your introduction and then how you will handle their most likely responses. You should write your script how you would say it and then practise it. The best way is through role play with a friend, colleague, manager or coach. Your script will evolve once you start using it but at least all your calls will be consistent.

Avoiding gatekeepers

Many salespeople fear and hate 'gatekeepers' who block them from getting through to the decision maker. Remember, these people are just doing their job of shielding their boss from people they think will be a waste of time. Treat gatekeepers with respect and they can make selling considerably easier for you. Once they can see that you are not going to be wasting their boss's time, they will treat you differently and normally be supportive and accommodating. Gatekeepers can also be a useful source of information when you are trying to understand how decisions are made and who the best people to speak to are.

COACHING SESSION 32

Which mistakes do you make?

- No compelling business reason ☐
- Sounding like a salesperson ☐
- Asking for a face-to-face meeting ☐
- Lack of scripting ☐
- Avoiding gatekeepers ☐

FINDING A COMPELLING BUSINESS REASON

Unless the people you are calling are actively in buying mode for the products and services you offer, then, at best, they will tell you when to call back but more often than not they will just avoid the call. Rather than engaging in tricks and lying to get through, it is better to work on your messaging and find a good reason for your call. The problem with lying to gatekeepers is that the caller is often found out and from then on is unlikely to get any further. It is much better to have a compelling reason why the person you are calling will want to speak to you.

A good reason to call would be offering fresh ideas about a particular business problem you are able to fix. When you are calling, you want to know two things:

1. Do they have the business problem?

2. Do they want to fix it?

This is a different type of call from asking whether they are interested in buying your product or service because if they have the problem then they may learn something by speaking to you.

For example, if you are selling HR consultancy services and you are targeting business owners who are worried about being taken to an employment tribunal, then your compelling business reason for calling could be to offer fresh ideas about avoiding employment tribunals.

There are several ways in which you could deliver these fresh ideas, including:

- a special report

- an event

- a webinar

- a free consultation.

The point is that the focus of attention is on the topic of avoiding employment tribunals and not your products and services. People may be more willing to start a conversation about the relevant topic than they are about talking about HR consultancy services and yet, once they start to discuss their issues, they could very well end up talking to you about your HR consulting services.

The thing that makes cold calling easier with this approach is that you start the relationship off in a way that eventually leads to you being seen as a trusted adviser, you find out whether they have the underlying problem, and even if they do not have an interest in talking about the problem, you leave the door open to call them again in the future about a different problem.

COACHING SESSION 33

What could you use as a compelling business reason to call?

1.

2.

3.

4.

YOUR INTRODUCTION SCRIPT

Your introduction script is what you say as soon as you are put through to the right person. You have just 10 to 15 seconds while the person decides how to handle the call and so it is worth working on your introduction script. At a normal pace, 15 seconds equates to about 40 words.

Example

Hi, my name is Richard and I am calling from The Accidental Salesman. We provide business development masterclasses for consultants and trusted advisers and I just wondered if you are open to fresh ideas in relation to winning more business.

You should use the work you have done in Chapter 4 to determine the essential information to get into your 15-second pitch.

😕😕 COACHING SESSION 34

Write out your 15-second pitch.

_____

_____

_____

_____

_____

RESPONSE SCRIPTS

Once you have delivered your 15-second pitch, you will get a variety of responses, including 'Tell me more!' Your response scripts give you a way of handling the most common responses. Here are a few examples with possible responses.

'Too busy'

This response is normally words to the effect of 'Sorry, I am too busy – can you call back later?'

There is a high chance that anyone you call will be busy and so you will probably get this response a lot. Your answer might be something like:

'That's OK – When would be a good time to call?'

'Send information'

This one is ambiguous because it sounds as if they may be interested but actually they are probably too busy to take the call and it is a stock response. Your answer might be something like:

'That's OK, would you mind answering a couple of questions so I can send you the right information?'

They will either come back and say they are too busy, in which case you can use the 'Too busy' response or they will allow you to ask them a couple of questions.

'Happy with supplier'

This one is interesting. If you take the 'fresh ideas' approach, you will rarely have a problem with this one.

What they are saying is that, whatever you are offering, they will be buying from their existing supplier. The truth is that most people you call will probably be happy with their existing supplier until they are not! If they think you are going to give some fresh insights, they may still like to speak to you anyway – just to get the insights. Your answer might be something like:

'That's OK – we offer something unique and I am just calling to see if you are open to fresh ideas in relation to .... I would only need a few moments of your time.'

Few people will admit that they are not open to fresh ideas and most decision makers will be prepared to invest a few minutes if it could be of use in solving their business problems.

'We do not have any budget at the moment'

This is another one you will get from time to time. They do not yet know what you are selling but, whatever it is, they cannot afford it! If you get this a lot, you may need to adjust your 15-second pitch.

'That's OK. Most people we speak to do not have a specific budget when we call. I am just calling to see if you are open to fresh ideas in relation to .... I would only need a few moments of your time.'

If they have the problem and it is worth them fixing it, then they will find the budget.

'Tell me more!'

You need to be especially ready for this one. You should respond with your pitch followed by a request to arrange a ten-minute telephone conversation and an offer to send some information after that conversation. You should be prepared for them to want to proceed straight to the ten-minute telephone conversation.

COACHING SESSION 35

In the table below, write the ten most common responses to your introduction and then your answer.

Number	Response	Answer
1.		
2.		
3.		
4.		
5.		
6.		
7.		
8.		
9.		
10.		

CALL BACKS

One of the unfortunate truths of cold calling is that you will probably have to call people back several times before you get the opportunity for a conversation. This is why the results of cold calling increase over time. If you only ever call once, then the time spent on getting through would have been wasted. It is better to use a CRM system or a spreadsheet and keep track of the calls you have made and schedule a reminder to call back.

When you call, you probably have a 20 per cent chance, on average, that the person you call is able to take your call. Then, when you are put through, there is a large chance that they are in the middle of some kind of work and not in a right frame of mind to take the call. Expect to make call backs many times. It does not take long to make a call where there is little conversation. It is persistence that produces much of the results from cold calling.

When you do persist, you get the advantage of timing and familiarity. When you are able to deliver your 15-second pitch and occasionally a longer pitch, your contact becomes familiar with what you do and, when circumstances change, you will be one of the people they remember. As long as you are friendly, they will admire your persistence too. The great thing is that you will not need to keep buying new prospect details. A database of about 500 to 1,000 of well-targeted contacts called regularly should be enough to generate a regular supply of sales leads.

Ultimately, unless someone you call asks you not to call them again, you can assume that they are OK for you to call back.

The information provided above is based on business-to-business calling. In the UK there is a telephone preference service and many countries have something similar where people can register that they do not want to receive cold calls. You should make sure that you regularly check your list against this service to make sure you are not contravening any local regulations.

🗣🗣 COACHING SESSION 36

How do you plan to manage your call list and call backs?

1. _____

2. _____

3. _____

4. _____

5. _____

6. _____

7. _____

8. _____

→ NEXT STEPS

Now that we have started to generate more sales leads of better quality, it is time to look at getting better at converting those sales leads into cash in the bank. This will be the focus of Part 2 of this book, 'Closing the sale'.

TAKEAWAYS

What have I learned?

1. What is a compelling business reason and why is it important to have one when cold calling?

_____

_____

_____

_____

_____

_____

_____

_____

_____

_____

_____

_____

2. What is the purpose of scripting and what parts of the cold call are most important to script?

_____

_____

_____

_____

_____

_____

_____

_____

_____

_____

_____

_____

3. Why do call backs increase the effectiveness of cold calling?

_____

_____

_____

_____

_____

_____

_____

_____

_____

_____

_____

_____

_____

_____

_____

_____

_____

_____

_____

_____

_____

_____

PART 2
CLOSING THE SALE

THE PROCESS OF SELLING

- Understand the process of closing a sale
- Know how to qualify your sales leads
- Create exit criteria for each stage of your sales process

 COACHING SESSION 37

Self-assessment

Assessment criteria	Score
I follow a documented, multi-stage sales process to close a sale.	
I know the tasks that need to be completed at each stage of my sales process and what is required before passing on to the next stage.	
I never progress a sales opportunity until I have completed the current stage.	
I qualify every sales lead to ensure that it is a suitable sales opportunity.	
I have specific qualification questions which are answered prior to arranging a meeting.	
TOTAL	

Score yourself between 1 and 5. A score of 5 means this statement is totally true; 1 means this statement is totally untrue. Total up your score. The maximum is 25 out of 25. Even if you give yourself a full score, I recommend you complete this chapter.

THE PROCESS OF CONSULTATIVE SELLING

If you have experience in sales, you will have noticed that each sales opportunity will go through an evolutionary progress, from the prospect first being interested to them agreeing to buy your products and services. While each sales opportunity might be very different, the process each sales opportunity goes through is similar.

When we are looking to win more sales opportunities, we need to start paying attention to the sales process. The more we are in control of our sales process, the more control we have over each sale and of reaching our sales targets.

There are seven logical stages in the consultative sales process:

Stage	Stage	Purpose
1.	Generate interest	To get specific members of our target audience to express an interest in having a conversation
2.	Qualify interest	To confirm that this is a suitable sales opportunity
3.	Discover the problem	To discover the information required to be able to propose a solution
4.	Propose your solution	To propose and sell your solution
5.	Negotiate the solution	To refine the solution and agree terms
6.	Conclude the sale	To get formal agreement to proceed
7.	Deliver the solution	To deliver what was agreed

Stage 7 is critical and often overlooked. As we learned from Part 1 of this book, getting customers to spend more with us and refer us to their trusted contacts is what makes sales much easier. Therefore it is vital that we ensure that we only sell what can be delivered and – once we have made the sale – that it is delivered.

In this part of the book we will be looking at the stages of the sales process in more detail because small refinements to what you do at each stage of the sales process can have a big impact on the results you get. While many classic sales books put an emphasis on techniques for closing the sale, which happens towards the end of the sales process, getting the earlier stages right normally has a much bigger impact on winning more sales.

♀♀ COACHING SESSION 38

Fill in the missing words.

Paying attention to the _____ my sales opportunities go through will give me

more _____ over each sale and help me achieve my overall sales _____.

GARBAGE IN, GARBAGE OUT

'Garbage in, garbage out' is a well-worn phrase in software development. You can have an amazing piece of software, but unless you enter in the right kind of data you are unlikely to get the results you were expecting. The same is true with your sales process. You need to ensure that you put the right kind of opportunities into your sales process and be prepared to stop the sales process as soon as you believe that you are unlikely to win the sale. The reason this is important is that the further you go down the sales process the more time you need to invest in the sales opportunity.

Here is a breakdown of the time you might spend on each stage of the selling process:

Stage	Activity	Average time spent
Qualify interest	A brief telephone conversation	10 minutes
Discover problem	One or more meetings with the prospect to discuss their issues. Often this will include travel.	3 hours
Propose solution	Putting together a proposal	4 hours
Negotiate solution	Refining the proposal	30 minutes
Conclude the sale	Drawing up the contract	10 minutes

As we can see from the above typical example, it takes roughly one full day of effort, over time, to win a sales opportunity once the prospect has expressed an interest. If the sales opportunity is not a good fit, it does not make sense to pursue that sales opportunity. Rather than investing a day in a sales opportunity we are unlikely to ever win, we would be better served spending that day finding sales opportunities that are a good fit and likely to turn into a sale.

After making a short check to ensure a good fit, you can have the confidence to invest the time into doing the discovery part of the sales process. While you proceed through the discovery process, you continue to ensure that this is an opportunity you can win. Again, there is no point investing time in writing a sales proposal if you do not believe you will win the sale.

⚉ COACHING SESSION 39

Fill in the missing words.

Qualifying interest is about saving _____. I will win more sales when

I _____ poor-quality _____ _____ from

my sales process and invest the time I save in generating quality _____

_____ rather than trying to close opportunities that are unlikely to lead to a sale.

QUALIFYING INTEREST

We have seen that the qualify interest stage of the sales process is about being in control of your time. In addition to avoiding wasted time on poor-quality sales opportunities, it can also save time by getting some details prior to entering the discovery phase of the sales process.

You will need to decide what information you require before advancing to the discovery phase. Here are some examples:

Information required	Purpose
Why did they express an interest?	This is normally the first piece of information you should seek so that you can understand their motive and assess whether they match one of your customer archetypes.
Do they have an existing supplier?	If they have a current supplier, you need to know why they are talking to additional suppliers. This will give you more insights into their buying motives.
Who will be involved in making the buying decision?	You need to understand who you should be speaking to at the discovery stage. You may need to speak to more than one person.
Do they have sufficient budget?	You need to know whether they are going to have an issue with your pricing.
What are their timescales?	You need to know what stage they are at in their buying process.

I recommend that, for each piece of information you require, you script out the precise question you will ask so that it fits your circumstances and your style of language.

Why did they express an interest?

Finding out why someone is interested may seem like a strange question to ask but it reveals a lot about the motive of the person expressing the interest. You will find out whether they are just curious, whether they are actively researching a solution to a problem, or whether they are actually already in buying mode and talking to other potential suppliers.

While you want to know the reason why they have expressed an interest, your question should be something a little less direct. For example:

- 'I know it sounds like a funny question but do you mind me asking what led you to make the enquiry?'

- 'Do you mind me asking what you are looking to achieve?'

- 'I am interested in knowing why you are interested in _____.'

If appropriate, you may want to ask a supplementary question about why they are interested now, especially if you have been talking to them over a period of time and they have only just expressed an interest.

👥 COACHING SESSION 40

Script out how you will discover why they are interested.

1. _____
2. _____
3. _____
4. _____
5. _____
6. _____
7. _____

Do they have an existing supplier?

What you hope to hear is that they either do not have a current supplier or they have a good reason for wanting to work with someone different. For example, their existing supplier may have let them down or they may be looking for a specialist.

A big sales time waster is where prospects are just in the market for the sole purpose of negotiating better rates with their existing supplier. Unless there is a good reason for a prospect to change supplier, it is safe to assume that they will not – unless a competitor can offer something significantly better.

On the other hand, they may have already spent money trying to solve the problem without success or they may not have got on with the supplier. This is very useful information that a prospective customer will rarely volunteer without being asked. Yet it will provide you with valuable insights about whether to progress the sale and in which direction.

Examples of questions you could ask include:

- 'What have you done about this already?'
- 'Who has previously been supplying you?'
- 'Who currently supplies this for you?'

Even if you find out that they are just comparing prices, you may decide to progress to the discovery phase anyway, in the hope that you will find some problems with their existing supplier. It is a judgement call and it is better for you to go into the discovery process with your eyes wide open and get the chance to decline if you think it will be a waste of your time and the incumbent supplier will just match your price.

🗣🗣 COACHING SESSION 41

Script out how you will discover whether they have an existing supplier.

1. _____

2. _____

3. _____

4. _____

Who will be involved in making the buying decision?

A common mistake people make when attempting to qualify a sales opportunity is to ask the person they are speaking to whether they are the decision maker. Invariably, the answer you will get to this question is 'Yes'. Often, people think they are the one who makes the decision but, for your purposes, you need to know who will make the ultimate decision as well as those who will be a strong influence on the final decision. This is so that you can understand how the decision will ultimately be made and who you need to speak to during the discovery stage of the sales process.

🗣🗣 COACHING SESSION 42

Script out how you will discover who will be involved in making the buying decision.

1. _____

2. _____

3. _____

4. _____

5. _____

Do they have sufficient budget?

Another common mistake is to ask a prospect directly about their budget during the very first conversation. What often happens is that the person you are speaking to will tell you they do not have a budget or that they would prefer not to say. At this stage in the process, it is more important that we check that budget will not be an issue than knowing the exact amount.

Examples of questions you could ask include:

- 'Our packages start at £5,000 – will that be an issue?'

- 'Our packages range from £5,000 through to £100,000 – will that be an issue?'

- 'What is the most you would be prepared to spend on this?'

COACHING SESSION 43

Script out how you will discover whether they have sufficient budget.

1. _____

2. _____

3. _____

4. _____

5. _____

What are their timescales?

The timing of the opportunity is also important. You want to know whether there is a specific requirement and also when they would be looking to make a decision. At this early stage it does not need to be precise. If you ask when they are likely to make a decision, you will often get a vague response because, in reality, they may not know. However, they should have a sense of whether it will be in the short term or longer term.

Examples of questions to elicit this information include:

- 'When are you looking to move forward on this? Is it sooner or later?'

- 'When are you looking to implement this? Will it be in the next few months or longer term?'

- 'How urgent is this? Is it something you are looking to do quickly or something longer term?'

COACHING SESSION 44

Script out how you will discover their timescales.

1. ____________________
2. ____________________
3. ____________________
4. ____________________
5. ____________________

CLOSING EACH STAGE

Rather than focusing all our attention on closing the sale, we should instead be looking at closing each stage of the sales process one by one. We should be aware of the specific tasks we need to do at each stage of the sales process and what specific evidence we require to confirm that the stage has been completed and that we are ready to move on to the next stage.

We want specific exit criteria which are, in effect, a test to show that a sales opportunity is ready to move from one stage of the sales process to the next. We also need to recognize that some sales opportunities will falter and be eliminated because they are unable to move beyond a certain stage. This is normal and as long as we are clear about what we need to do at each stage of the sales process and about our exit criteria, we remain in control.

Example

Stage	Tasks	Exit criteria
Generate interest	Carry out lead generation activity.	A ten-minute initial telephone call has been diarized.
Qualify interest	Discover buying motives and timescales, and check that price will not be an issue.	Customer fit is confirmed and an invitation to a discovery meeting has been diarized.
Discover the problem	Meet with key influencers of the decision, to discover information required to win the sale.	Enough information has been gathered to produce a proposal.

Stage	Tasks	Exit criteria
Propose your solution	Create and deliver a compelling proposal.	Proposal is delivered and acknowledged.
Negotiate the solution	Shape the solution where appropriate and overcome any objections and reservations. Agree T&Cs.	Revised proposal and verbal agreement to go ahead.
Conclude the sale	Get a purchase order and payment.	Payment received.
Deliver the solution	Deliver agreed solution.	Customer review.

Depending on what you are selling and who you are selling to, your process tasks and exit criteria may be similar or, indeed, completely different. It is important that you clarify what tasks you need to do at each stage of your sales process and how you will know everything is complete.

COACHING SESSION 45

List your tasks and exit criteria for each stage of your sales process.

Stage	Tasks	Exit criteria
Generate interest		
Qualify interest		
Discover the problem		
Propose your solution		
Negotiate the solution		
Conclude the sale		
Deliver the solution		

ANSWER TO COACHING SESSION 38

Paying attention to the process my sales opportunities go through will give me more control over each sale and help me achieve my overall sales targets.

ANSWER TO COACHING SESSION 39

Qualifying interest is about saving time. I will win more sales when I qualify out poor quality sales opportunities from my sales process and invest the time I save in generating quality sales opportunities rather than trying to close opportunities that are unlikely to lead to a sale.

NEXT STEPS

Now that we understand our sales process and how to qualify interest, we need to learn how to discover enough information to write a compelling proposal.

👍 TAKEAWAYS

What have I learned?

1. Why is it important to be in control of your sales process?

_____

_____

_____

_____

_____

_____

_____

_____

_____

2. What is the main purpose of qualifying interest?

_____

_____

_____

_____

_____

_____

_____

_____

_____

_____

3. In the context of your sales process, what are exit criteria and what role do they play?

8 DISCOVERING NEEDS AND WANTS

 OUTCOMES FROM THIS CHAPTER

- Understand why it is important to avoid 'selling' during the discovery stage
- Know what information you need to discover
- Learn a methodology for discovering the information

COACHING SESSION 46

Self-assessment

Assessment criteria	Score
I use a methodology for my sales meetings.	
I always discover the outcome my prospects are seeking to achieve.	
I always discover what my prospects are seeking to change, and why.	
I always discover what impact the change is likely to have on my prospects and also the impact of maintaining the status quo.	
I always discover whether my prospective customers have any specific requirements and constraints that will have an impact on my proposed solution.	
TOTAL	

Score yourself between 1 and 5. A score of 5 means this statement is totally true; 1 means this statement is totally untrue. Total up your score. The maximum is 25 out of 25. Even if you give yourself a full score, I recommend you complete this chapter.

THE FOUR ESSENTIAL ELEMENTS OF DISCOVERY

The objective of the discovery stage of the sales process is to find out enough information to create a compelling sales proposal. A critical part of the consultative sales process is therefore not only to gather information to formulate your proposed solution but also to discover how to pitch your solution.

It is at this stage that things normally go wrong. One of the biggest traps is treating discovery meetings as 'sales meetings'. The problem is that we spend valuable time with the prospect trying to sell them something rather than taking the time to build trust and discover enough information about their problems that will help know what and how we should be selling to them. The discovery stage of the sales process is about questioning and listening. If you ask the right questions and listen to the answers, your prospective customer will tell you how best to sell your solution when the time comes.

It's a bit like going to the doctor with a medical problem. You clearly know what the symptoms are and you may have an idea of what kind of medicine you need, but a good doctor will still ask you some questions and, perhaps, even do some basic tests, to satisfy themselves that they are able to make a correct diagnosis. The discovery stage is about diagnosis and not prescription. The great thing is that if we approach this stage in the right way, our prospects will tell us how to win the sale.

In the discovery stage of the sales process there are four key pieces of information that we need to discover in order to be able to produce a compelling sales proposal:

- Goal information
- Reality information
- Impact information
- Needs information

It is important to understand that we do not need to discover these elements in sequence. We just need to ensure that we have gathered all four elements of information in sufficient detail during the discovery stage. In some cases, a prospect will be fairly clear what they want and so starting with goal makes sense. In other cases, a prospect may just have a problem with no sense of what a solution looks like. In these circumstances, you would begin by understanding the reality and impact before working on the goal.

As we go through the detail of each element there will be an exercise for you to do on that element. I will use a common example for each element and then you will be asked to do something similar based on a recent, or current, sales opportunity. Please use the same sales opportunity for each element.

Goal information

Discovering goal information is about discovering more about our prospect's buying motives and in particular what they are seeking to achieve. We want to get a clear understanding of their expected outcome and what success looks like for them. For example, if we were selling website development, the goal element of discovery would be about finding out what they hope to achieve as a result of redeveloping their website rather than what they want their website to look like. One prospect may be seeking to generate more sales leads for their business while another may just be going through a rebranding exercise and looking for their website to fit in with the new corporate image.

In some cases, your prospect may be so focused on a problem that they have not even thought about what they want to achieve. You can add real value to the sales process and start to build trust and confidence in your solution by helping them to clarify in their mind what success might look like to them once they have solved the problem. This will be done by asking questions and perhaps giving examples of what they could reasonably expect to achieve.

Example

Here is an abbreviated example of what the notes for the **goal** element of discovery for an accounting software package might look like.

GOAL

The Managing Director (MD), John Smith, wants an accounting software package that is going to enable him to get his management information more quickly. It currently takes his accounting team nearly a month to produce his management pack and they are telling him it is because of the accounting system. He wants a monthly management pack on his desk on the fifth working day of each month without fail, so that he feels in control of the finances and can make faster decisions.

The Finance Director (FD), Sophie Goodall, wants her department to be able to cope with increasing demands for financial information without increasing headcount. In addition to producing the management pack by the fifth working day of each month, Sophie wants to be able to quickly turn around the increasing number of ad-hoc requests for financial information which are currently slowing her team down. Sophie wants minimum disruption during the transition to a new system.

COACHING SESSION 47

Using a recent or current discovery meeting, write out their goal element.

_____

_____

_____

_____

_____

_____

Reality information

Reality information relates to your prospect's current situation and the problem they are trying to solve. In order to provide a solution, you need to know about the problem they will be expecting you to solve. You are seeking to understand as much as possible about the background to their current situation and the problems they are faced with. For example, continuing with the website example, if they were looking for their new website to generate more sales leads, you might be asking about how many sales leads they are currently generating. You would also be asking about website traffic to their website and what kind of analysis they have done on visitors to their site. Other reality information you might ask would be things like who has previously worked on their website and why they feel the need to speak to other web development companies. Delving even deeper, we may want to discover other sources of sales leads and how they track where their sales leads come from.

So far, we have been discovering goal and reality information and we have not been trying to sell anything. What we are seeking to do is establish a clear gap between what they want and what they currently have. In other words, if they are not looking for anything different from what they are currently doing, why would they want to change? If they were looking to get a better price, then that would come out during your questions here.

If the whole sales opportunity is about them paying less for the same service and you have decided to pursue the opportunity, then, in addition to finding out more about what service they currently get as well as what they are currently paying, you would need to find out what they would want to be paying in order to consider making the change. You need to be able to ask direct questions and if they are not prepared to be open with you, you may be wasting your time.

Example

Here is an abbreviated example of what the notes for the **reality** element of discovery for an accounting software package might look like.

REALITY

The MD John Smith is relatively new to his position and struggling to understand the cost base of the company. He gets a monthly pack of management information which arrives at the end of the month, or even later. It does not give him much detail and he is frustrated at how long it takes to get any answers to seemingly simple financial questions. He has friends who are running similar-sized companies and they automatically get all the information they need within five working days, with fewer people. John recognizes that the accounting system is prehistoric and is willing to invest in something more up to date.

The FD Sophie Goodall is under great stress coping with the demand for information. The previous MD was fairly relaxed about things and she is finding it hard to keep up with the new MD's demands for information. The accounting system has a fixed set of reports and they have to get a consultant in at £500 per day every time they want any additional reports.

Sophie has two full-time financial assistants working for her.

░░ COACHING SESSION 48

Using a recent or current discovery meeting, write out their reality element.

_____

_____

_____

_____

_____

Impact information

The next element of discovery is to find out the impact on your prospect of changing from their current reality to their goal. This information is essential for beginning to understand how your prospect will benefit from making the change. We also want to discover the impact on your prospect of not making the change and maintaining the status quo. Continuing with our web development example, we may discover that each sale is worth, on average, £10,000 and they are not currently generating any sales leads from their website. If they were to achieve their goal of one sale a month coming from their website, the impact would be £120,000 per year. You may also discover that the business is only currently making a small profit and an extra £120,000 would have a considerable impact on the business going forward.

It is important to ask questions about future impact because in many cases your prospect's circumstances may change in the future. They may have a problem that they can currently tolerate but that will become intolerable in the future. In the same way as much insurance is sold on the basis of avoiding a problem in the future, it is important to not just talk about the benefits of achieving their goal but also about what would happen if things remain as they are.

With impact questions we start to get a sense of the value we are able to add with our solution. This is important when it comes to presenting the price of our solution. We need to be able to show that the value the prospect will get from our solution is greater than the cost we are asking them to pay. Otherwise, why would they want to go ahead? This task becomes much easier if you get the prospect to tell you the impact. Then when you do your proposal you are merely playing back what they have already told you. And if you decide that you are unable to provide enough value, it is time to start thinking about withdrawing from the sales process and not wasting time writing a proposal.

Example

Here is an abbreviated example of what the notes for the **impact** element of discovery for an accounting software package might look like.

IMPACT

John Smith reckons he will be able to reduce the cost base of the business by 10 per cent once he has a better understanding of the costs. That will save £100,000 per year.

Sophie Goodall's department, is currently spending £2,000 per month on reports for ad-hoc information, which will be saved.

Once the system is fully up and running, Sophie is hoping that she will need only one financial assistant working on the accounts and she plans to get the other financial assistant to work on helping her with budgeting and forecasting.

COACHING SESSION 49

Using a recent or current discovery meeting, write out their impact element.

_____

_____

_____

_____

_____

Needs information

Sometimes a prospect may have a reasonable idea of what they want to buy. Others may just have specific requirements that need to be met or certain constraints that need to be accommodated. We need to take note of these specific needs when we are formulating our proposed solution. Needs would also include any known constraints such as timing or budget.

Continuing with our web development example, the prospect's specific requirements may be that they want to be able to make updates to the website themselves and they want the website to include a blog. The prospect wants the website ready before they do an exhibition in three months' time and they have a maximum initial budget of £5,000. When they start to see a return on the website, a larger budget could be available.

The needs aspect of discovery should always be the last area to focus on rather than the first. Once you have discussed the goal, reality and impact aspects with your prospect, they will be much clearer about any specific needs. The point is that your facilitating them through the thinking could end up changing what they think they need.

Example

Here is an abbreviated example of what the notes for the needs element of discovery for an accounting software package might look like.

NEEDS

The FD Sophie Goodall wants the accounting package to be simple enough that the MD can run his own ad-hoc reports and 'drill down' into the detail if necessary. He needs to be able to do this when away from the office.

Sophie wants to reduce the effort it takes to produce the monthly information. The company is aiming to expand in the future through acquisitions and she also wants a system that can cope with adding additional companies. She is looking for a 'software as a service' model because they cannot afford any large capital expenditure.

Sophie would like assistance in migrating from their existing system and also some training for her team.

COACHING SESSION 50

Using a recent or current discovery meeting, write out their needs element.

_____

_____

_____

_____

_____

→ NEXT STEPS

This chapter has been about giving you a methodology for gathering information during the discovery stage of your sales process. In the next chapter we will work on improving your questioning and listening skills so that you find it easier to get the information you need.

👍 TAKEAWAYS

What have I learned?

1. What are you seeking to discover with goal information?

_____

_____

_____

_____

_____

_____

_____

_____

_____

_____

_____

2. What are you seeking to discover with reality information?

_____

_____

_____

_____

_____

_____

_____

_____

_____

_____

_____

3. What are you seeking to discover with impact information?

_____

_____

_____

_____

_____

_____

_____

_____

_____

4. What are you seeking to discover with needs information?

_____

_____

_____

_____

_____

_____

_____

_____

_____

9 QUESTIONING AND LISTENING

 OUTCOMES FROM THIS CHAPTER

- Avoid common questioning and listening mistakes
- Control the amount of detail you get from your questions
- Improve your listening skills

COACHING SESSION 51

Self-assessment

Assessment criteria	Score
In discovery meetings my prospective customers always talk more than I do.	
I prepare for my discovery and consider the questions I need to ask to gain the information I need.	
I carefully phrase my questions to ensure that the answer has the right level of detail for my needs.	
I listen carefully to the answers to my questions and my prospective customers can see that I am listening.	
I 'listen' to body language in response to my questions and not just the words used.	
TOTAL	

Score yourself between 1 and 5. A score of 5 means this statement is totally true; 1 means this statement is totally untrue. Total up your score. The maximum is 25 out of 25. Even if you give yourself a full score, I recommend you complete this chapter.

COMMON MISTAKES WITH QUESTIONING AND LISTENING DURING THE DISCOVERY STAGE

Questioning and listening are essential for staying in control of the sales process. Here are some of the most common mistakes that salespeople make in relation to questioning and listening:

Asking too many questions

The objective of the discovery meeting is to gather important information rather than ask questions. It is much better to ask a few carefully chosen questions that get the prospect talking freely than to make the prospect feel as if they are being interrogated.

Asking too many closed questions

Some people habitually ask questions that can only be answered with a 'yes' or 'no' response. Such questions are commonly referred to as 'closed questions'. While closed questions have a very important role to play in confirming information, they are not very effective at extracting information. For example:

- **Closed question:** 'Do you have an existing supplier?'
- **Open question:** 'How do you currently get your supplies?'

We need to be thinking about the information we require and then pose the question that will give us that information.

Asking leading questions

This is where the salesperson skilfully phrases questions to manipulate the prospect into saying what the salesperson wants to hear. Their objective is to pave the way for a well-rehearsed sales pitch. The problem with this approach is that the salesperson is missing out on valuable information that would make their pitch more effective. In addition, their prospect is often aware of what is happening, which leads to them becoming guarded.

Not listening to the answers

Sometimes a salesperson is so focused on what they are going to say next that they are not listening to the answer to the previous question! We need to go into our discovery meetings knowing what information we require and which questions will get us that information. This is so that we can concentrate on what is being said and be able to ask supplementary questions for gaining additional clarity.

Ignoring body language

When we communicate with one another we give away subtle clues about what we are thinking through our tone of voice, our posture and other, more subtle things like facial features and skin tone. In addition to listening to the words spoken, we should be 'listening' to what the body language is saying. The words should always be interpreted in the context of the body language.

COACHING SESSION 52

Which mistakes do you currently make?

- Asking too many questions ☐
- Asking too many closed questions ☐
- Asking leading questions ☐
- Not listening to the answers ☐
- Ignoring body language ☐

CLOSED QUESTIONS

The definition of a closed question is one where the answer can only be 'Yes' or 'No'.	TRUE/FALSE

The correct answer is FALSE. While a question that can only be answered 'Yes' or 'No' is an example of a closed question, closed questions are where the range of available answers is limited. For example, 'What would you like to drink – tea or coffee?' is a closed question because the range of answers has been limited to tea and coffee. Indeed, the following would also be a closed question: 'What would you like to drink – tea, coffee or water?'

Closed questions are important in the discovery stage of the sales process to confirm our understanding of what the prospect has told us. For example, 'Am I correct in understanding that ... ?' You may also want to use a closed question if you need to make a choice before proceeding with a line of enquiry. For example: 'Which is more important to you ...?'

And, of course, we use closed questions to get our prospect to make a decision. 'Would you be happy to proceed on that basis?'

🗪🗪 COACHING SESSION 53

Fill in the missing words.

When we ask closed questions we give our prospects a limited number of available

_____. Closed questions are useful for _____ information and

getting a _____.

OPEN QUESTIONS

I like to think of open questions as 'open-ended questions' because we should be removing any restrictions we place on the answers we receive. We want to discover what is on our prospect's mind and to do that we pose a question that will give us the specific information we require.

Classically open questions start with words like who, what, where, when and how.

Type	Information provided	Example
Who	People	'Who will be managing this project?'
What	Various	'What are the objectives of this project?' 'What have you achieved so far?'
Where	Location	'Where will the project team be based?'
When	Timing	'When does the project need to be completed?'
How	Process	'How will you be managing this project?'

However, just because a question begins with one of the above types, this does not mean that the question is open-ended. Consider this question:

'When does the project need to be completed? Will it be this year or next year?'

By immediately tagging a closed supplementary question on the end of an open question, the answer will no longer be open-ended. In this example there are now only two possible answers.

However, if your intent is to discover more information than this, you could ask a question that is technically closed and yet, through your voice intonation, still conveys to the prospect that you are expecting more than just a yes or no answer.

The bottom line is that when you are clear about the information you require and in control of the questions you ask, you will begin to be in control of the sale.

COACHING SESSION 54

Fill in the missing words.

_____ questions will enable me to gather the information I need to

discover and I will use _____ questions to confirm my understanding.

CONTROLLING DETAIL

Many senior executives communicate in big-picture terms, which is useful when we want to gain an overview but can be frustrating when we are seeking to gain more detail. Others can be very vague with their answers and, at times like these, we need a way of tactfully asking for more detail and precision. Thankfully, the technique is very simple. All we need to do is add a single word like 'specifically' or 'exactly' to our question, For example:

Salesperson: 'Why are you looking to change supplier?'

Prospect: 'I am not happy with the service.'

Salesperson: 'What specific aspects of the service were you unhappy with?'

Prospect: 'Where do I begin? For a start, they always take ages to respond to a request ...'

At the other extreme, some people answer open questions with too much detail and we need a way of tactfully getting them to provide less detail. We do this by prefacing the question with a phrase like 'Taking a step back ...' For example:

Prospect: 'We have been looking at various products like ...'

Salesperson: 'Just taking a step back for a second, what are you aiming to achieve by using one of these products?'

Alternative prefaces include phrases like 'Looking at the bigger picture ...' or 'In terms of your overall objectives ...'

People who like detail will often use technical jargon, internal phraseology or acronyms that you have not heard before. If you are discussing an important area then make sure you understand the meaning of any abbreviations that your prospect may use or you may miss something important. For example:

Prospect: 'We plan to include this in our next sprint.'

Salesperson: 'When you say sprint, what do you mean specifically?'

Prospect: 'Oh, I'm sorry, it's a mini-project. It's part of our project management methodology.'

Some people will give you information that may sound like fact but which, on further investigation, turns out not to be true or not to be as clear cut as you were led to believe. When you hear the prospect using words like 'always' and 'never', alarm bells should start to ring. These are examples of generalizations and we need to challenge them to gain greater clarity. This is because, while the statement may be true some of the time, the words give the impression they are true *all* of the time. For example:

Salesperson: 'What specifically are you unhappy with?'

Prospect: 'They always take ages to respond to a request.'

Salesperson: 'Is that *every* single time or are there times when they respond promptly?'

Prospect: 'Well, to be fair, they are normally OK during office hours.'

In this example, the challenge to the generalization has clarified the issue from being about response times to being about the service they receive out of office hours.

COACHING SESSION 55

Fill in the missing words.

If I want to increase the amount of detail from my prospect, then I simply insert the

word _____ into my question.

If I want less detail, I insert the phrase _____ at

the _____ of the sentence.

PLANNING YOUR QUESTIONS

By now you should be clear about the type of information you want to gather during the discovery phase:

- Goal information
- Reality information
- Impact information
- Needs information

In the previous chapter we learned about what type of information is required for each of these four elements. When you ask the prospect questions they will give answers. However, we should be respecting the time of our prospect and our own time to make the discovery time as brief as possible. We need to think carefully, in advance of the meeting, about what we want to discover and what questions we should be asking.

When it comes to the discovery stage of the sales process, it is as if we are opening one of those combination locks you get on briefcases that require you to select several numbers. When we have all the numbers we will unlock the sale and, provided we ask the right questions, our prospect will give us the precise combination. I hope you can see that it is worth the effort to hone your questioning skills.

ᗢᗡ COACHING SESSION 56

For a specific opportunity, think about the information you want to discover for each of the four elements and then write down the questions you need to ask. Once you have all your questions written down, review the wording of the questions, one by one, to see whether they could be refined to make them more productive.

Element	Questions
Goal information	
Reality information	
Impact information	
Needs information	

ONLINE RESOURCE

Discovery

You can download a copy of the question planning sheet and meeting summary sheet from:

www.TYCoachbooks.com/Sales

DEVELOPING YOUR LISTENING SKILLS

If we are talking, we are not discovering. We need to ask our questions to direct the information our prospects give us and then we need to listen carefully to the answers. And when it comes to listening, the words that your prospect uses are only part of the story. We should be looking out for non-verbal clues that help us to understand the full meaning. Our prospect's body language can totally change the meaning of what they are saying or indicate things such as the fact that they are anxious, defensive, or simply that they have lost interest and are seeking to bring the meeting to a conclusion.

Body language and non-verbal communication is an entire study in itself and body language can differ between cultures and even between individual people within cultures. There is always the risk that we misread the signs. For example, a prospect folds their arms and we think they are getting defensive – when actually they are just feeling cold.

We should be looking out for changes in body language during our discovery meetings. In addition to looking at posture, we can also look at things like voice tone and quality, facial expressions and even skin tone, especially around the neck.

It can often be useful to raise body language observations with your prospect to aid the discovery process. For example:

Salesperson: 'I am sensing that you are a little confused by my question, would you like me to ask it in a different way?'

Prospect: 'Yes please; I was not sure what you meant by...'

Note taking

Many salespeople take a lot of notes during discovery meetings. While it is important to write down some critical information like numbers, the act of writing notes can affect our concentration which, in turn, can affect our ability to listen. I encourage you to start taking fewer notes during the discovery meeting and, instead, make sure you have time immediately after the meeting when you can make your notes for each of the four discovery elements. You will find that you pay much closer attention to body language and what is being said than you would if you were busy writing everything down. Taking fewer notes during a discovery meeting also applies where your discovery meeting is done by telephone. You will be amazed how much more information you gather when your attention is on discovering rather than note taking.

Role play

Role play is a great way to develop your skill at both asking good questions and listening to the answers you receive. The value of role play is in the feedback which enables us to fine-tune our approach without having to experiment with our prospects. Role play can help you find out what works and what does not work so that the words come naturally when you are with your prospects.

Another way to develop your questioning and listening skills is in social or work settings. During conversations with people, practise getting the other person to reveal information and practise directing the conversation and level of detail. You can do this by starting conversations with total strangers while waiting in a queue!

COACHING SESSION 57

Fill in the missing words.

I need to pay attention to body language because it can affect the _____ of

their answer. It can also give me insights into how they are _____.

ANSWER TO COACHING SESSION 53

When we ask closed questions we give our prospects a limited number of available answers. Closed questions are useful for confirming information and getting a decision.

ANSWER TO COACHING SESSION 54

Open questions will enable me to gather the information I need to discover and I will use closed questions to confirm my understanding.

ANSWER TO COACHING SESSION 55

If I want to increase the amount of detail from my prospect, then I simply add the word 'specifically' into my question.

If I want less detail, I insert the phrase 'taking a step back' at the beginning of the sentence.

ANSWER TO COACHING SESSION 57

I need to pay attention to body language because it can affect the meaning of their answer. It can also give me insights into what they are feeling.'

 ## NEXT STEPS

Now that we have all the information we need to propose our solution, it is time to start looking at how we will sell our solution.

👍 TAKEAWAYS

What have I learned?

1. What are open questions and what is their role in the discovery phase of the sales process?

_____

_____

_____

_____

_____

_____

_____

_____

2. What are closed questions and what is their role in the discovery phase of the sales process?

_____

_____

_____

_____

_____

_____

_____

_____

_____

_____

3. Why is it important to pay attention to body language during the discovery phase of the sales process?

_____

_____

_____

_____

_____

_____

_____

_____

_____

_____

_____

_____

_____

_____

_____

_____

_____

_____

_____

_____

_____

_____

10 MAKING YOUR PROPOSALS MORE COMPELLING

✔ OUTCOMES FROM THIS CHAPTER

- Avoid the common mistakes in making a proposal
- Understand the importance of a written proposal
- Know the important elements of a compelling proposal

 COACHING SESSION 58

Self-assessment

Assessment criteria	Score
My proposals make a compelling business case for buying my products and services.	
My proposals are structured and could be easily understood by someone who has not been involved in the sales process.	
The essence of my proposals can be summarized in a maximum of two pages.	
My proposals always include a summary of my prospect's motivation for change.	
My proposals always include a summary of why my prospect can trust my organization to deliver on the proposal.	
TOTAL	

Score yourself between 1 and 5. A score of 5 means this statement is totally true; 1 means this statement is totally untrue. Total up your score. The maximum is 25 out of 25. Even if you give yourself a full score, I recommend you complete this chapter.

MAKING THE BUSINESS CASE

With consultative selling, you do not start selling until you have completed the discovery stage of the sales process and it has become clear what the problem is and what, specifically, your prospect needs to buy. The real selling starts at the next stage, where you propose your solution. In a business-to-business context your proposal will almost always be a written document of some kind although, technically, a proposal could be delivered orally – for example, if you were doing consultative selling in a retail environment. For the purposes of this chapter I will be focusing on written proposals, whether you currently produce a formal document, a quote, or an email summarizing your proposed solution.

When reviewing proposals for clients, I come across many common mistakes including the following:

The proposal is too informal

Proposals contained within the body of an email should be avoided unless you use a formal template embedded within the email. The issue is that your prospect may also be talking to your competitors and there is the danger that your email proposal may look amateurish compared with theirs. My preference for short proposals would be to write a letter using your organization's letterhead and attach a soft copy of the letter to an email.

The proposal does not make a compelling business case

For me, the test of a good proposal is if someone who has not been involved in the sales process to date can understand the proposal and see that going ahead with the proposal makes sense. A common example is where you are unable to speak to the ultimate decision maker, despite trying. Alternatively, there could be other people involved in the decision behind the scenes, such as the finance director, a committee or even a spouse! In my experience, you cannot rely on other people to do your selling for you.

In effect, your proposal needs to be a selling document that will make your pitch for you and help your internal contacts make the business case, if necessary. It is a good discipline to get into because it gives a good reason for being thorough during the discovery stage of your sales process.

Not enough detail

Even though there may only be one ultimate decision maker, there could be more than one stakeholder with an influence on the final decision. This is especially the case when selling to larger organizations where decision making is often more complex. Given that your proposal is your sales pitch, the detail should cater for all the stakeholders with an influence and not just the ultimate decision maker.

Too much detail

I have seen many proposals that are just pages and pages of technical detail leaving out the essential element, which is making the business case. If your proposals need to be longer than a few pages, you should be thinking about doing an executive summary which contains the business case and put the detail in the main body of the document, as an appendix, or even in a separate document, referred to in the proposal.

Underselling the solution

You need to present your solution in its best light and this chapter of the book will show you what needs to be in your proposal to do that. Your competitor's solution may be inferior to yours but if they sell it better than you do then you risk losing the sale.

Overselling the solution

If you have followed the earlier stages of the consultative sales process and you have weeded out the sales opportunities that you are unlikely to win, you should be in with a good chance of success, provided you can present your case well. Proposals that exaggerate or are boastful risk the prospect becoming doubtful of the claims you are making. It is much better to make a business case for why your prospect needs to change and why your organization should be trusted to deliver the solution.

Lack of structure

You should assume that your sales proposal will not be studied in detail. On the contrary, it is more likely that readers will skim through the document. We need to make it easy for the reader to quickly assimilate key information and that is best done by having a logical structure and order to your document. It is good practice to get your proposals reviewed by someone who has not been involved in the sales process to ensure that they can follow the document and make sense of it.

COACHING SESSION 59

Which mistakes do you currently make?

- The proposal is too informal ☐
- The proposal does not make a compelling business case ☐
- Not enough detail ☐
- Too much detail ☐
- Underselling the solution ☐
- Overselling the solution ☐
- Lack of structure ☐

THE STRUCTURE OF A COMPELLING PROPOSAL

The primary function of a sales proposal is to make the business case and, while the specific contents of a written proposal may vary between organizations, there are certain key pieces of information that a proposal must contain. Moreover, the order of some of these pieces of information is critical. For example, your proposal needs to include costs and we should only talk about costs once we have established the need for change and presented what the prospect will be getting and its impact on their business.

When writing your sales proposals, I would like you to assume that it will be read by a cold-hearted finance director who needs to be convinced that they should release the budget. You need to get this finance director excited to know that, by spending this money, the business is going to be better off than it would be if they did nothing or choose a competitor's proposal.

There are some things that this cold-hearted finance director will want to know as they read through your proposal:

- What's it all about?
- What's the problem and why should I care?
- What do you intend to do about it?
- How much is it going to cost me?
- Why should I trust you to fix the problem for me?
- Where do we go from here?

Your proposal needs to be answering these questions in this order.

What's more, you need to be able to answer all those questions in one or two pages. Otherwise this finance director will just go straight to the costs and not bother reading the rest. Even though some of the readers of the proposal will be interested in the detail, this finance director is definitely not! They want a summary with more detailed information to back it up, if needed. This summary is often referred to as the 'Executive summary' but for simpler sales proposals it could just be a short letter.

What's it all about?

Your proposal needs to begin with a short and simple introduction that explains why you are writing it. In a letter or executive summary, it may just be a simple introductory sentence. In a longer proposal it would probably have a heading like:

- Introduction
- Background.

The purpose is to provide the reader with some context within which to interpret the proposal.

Example

Following on from our recent discussions regarding your sales growth plans, I am writing to outline how we can help you to generate more sales leads from your consulting team.

COACHING SESSION 60

Using a recent or current sales opportunity, write a short introduction for your proposal.

_____

_____

_____

_____

_____

What's the problem and why should I care?

This is a question that is often overlooked in proposals. The reader of a proposal needs to understand the business issues before they can assess the solution. In a proposal with headings, the heading would be something like 'Current situation'.

It may seem illogical to state the problem when the prospect has already given you the information anyway. There are two reasons for doing this:

- You are demonstrating to the prospect that you clearly understand the problem that they want you to fix and why fixing it is important to them.

- You are also providing context for anyone who has not been involved in the detailed sales discovery meetings.

This information should not be a surprise to anyone involved in your discovery process, although you may well articulate the problem better than they have been able to do up until now. For anyone else, they will get the high-level overview with more detail if they need it.

Example

As a business, XYZ are seeking significant sales growth, especially from existing customers. You want your technical consulting team to play an active part in this sales growth but previous attempts to train your consultants in sales techniques did not make any difference and led only to a rift between the consulting and sales teams.

COACHING SESSION 61

Using a recent or current sales opportunity, write a summary of the current situation, emphasizing the problem and why fixing the problem is important to them.

_____

_____

_____

_____

_____

What do you intend to do about it?

To answer this question, you need to put in a summary of your proposed solution, which should relate back to their current situation. Ideally, you should aim to end the section with a short sentence or two about how the customer will benefit from your proposed solution.

Example

Rather than trying to train your consultants into salespeople, we propose, as a first step, that we train your consultants to simply identify sales opportunities and initiate a discussion with the customer before bringing in the account manager to handle the sales opportunity in the normal way.

The training will be activity-based so that we develop your consultants' skill and confidence in identifying sales opportunities, initiating a conversation with customers, and paving the way for a conversation between the customer and the account manager. The training will be delivered by ex-consultants who your attendees will be able to relate to. I attach a draft outline of the training.

Following the training, we will facilitate a series of half-day workshops on a regional basis so that we can get your account managers and consultants to start focusing on working together to generate more sales leads from existing customers.

In order to realize the benefits of these trainings, we need to ensure that these new behaviours become 'business as usual'. This will require a coaching programme with the account managers and the consulting managers.

You mentioned that a sale would be worth an average of £25,000. Even if your 20 consultants initiate just one sale each over the course of a year, this will increase your annual revenue by £500,000. We also estimate that the impact in the second year will be even greater.

COACHING SESSION 62

Using a recent or current sales opportunity, write a summary of your proposed solution, emphasizing how this will solve their problem and the benefits they can expect.

_____

_____

_____

_____

_____

How much is it going to cost me?

Once you have reviewed the problem and your proposed solution, it is time to reveal how much the prospect will need to pay for your organization to solve the problem. The preceding paragraphs will give the reader something to measure the costs against.

Example

The cost of this programme will be £20,000 + VAT. [Also include details of specific terms e.g. expenses, payment terms, etc.]

😃😃 COACHING SESSION 63

Using a recent or current sales opportunity, write out the cost section for your proposal.

_____

_____

_____

_____

_____

Why should I trust you to fix the problem for me?

This section should focus on why the prospect should choose your organization to solve the problem for them. In Chapter 4 we looked at a product or service and how to craft your messages to show how it was different and relevant. This would be the place to include it in your proposal.

Specialist experience counts for a lot and, if you feel it will help, you can indicate that they can speak to one or two of your other customers. However, if you make a promise of customer introductions, you should be prepared to deliver on your promise.

Example

> The Accidental Salesman provides sales training for trusted advisers. We specialize in helping consultants engage more fully in the sales process. Our trainers are all ex-consultants who are not only highly skilled in consultative selling but also in helping consultants overcome sales reluctance and think differently about sales. The lead consultant we are proposing is Richard White and I attach a brief bio.
>
> We would be happy to introduce you to one or two of our existing customers if you would like to speak to them about our work.

COACHING SESSION 64

Using a recent or current sales opportunity, write out the cost section for your proposal.

_____

_____

_____

_____

_____

_____

_____

_____

_____

_____

_____

_____

_____

_____

_____

Where do we go from here?

Finally, your proposal should have a call to action that can normally be covered by a simple sentence or two explaining the next steps.

Example

We would love to work with you on this project. If you would like to proceed, then please confirm by email and we can get started on the planning.

COACHING SESSION 65

Using a recent or current sales opportunity, write a call to action for your proposal.

_____

_____

_____

_____

_____

_____

_____

_____

_____

_____

_____

_____

_____

_____

EXTRA INFORMATION IN YOUR PROPOSAL

The above proposal structure suggests the content recommended for the executive summary or proposal letter. Depending on what you are selling, you may include other information. For example, you may want to include information about:

- project deliverables

- project risks

- terms and conditions.

My recommendation is that you include this information in the main body of your proposal rather than in the executive summary. This will prevent the business case getting lost in the details.

 **NEXT STEPS**

Now that you have delivered a compelling sales proposal, in the next chapter we will be looking at how to conclude the sale.

TAKEAWAYS

What have I learned?

1. What is the purpose of a written sales proposal?

_____

_____

_____

_____

_____

_____

_____

_____

_____

_____

2. Why is the order of the content in a proposal important?

_____

_____

_____

_____

_____

_____

_____

_____

_____

_____

_____

3. Why is it important to include the current situation within a proposal?

_____

_____

_____

_____

_____

_____

_____

_____

_____

_____

_____

_____

_____

_____

_____

_____

_____

_____

_____

11 | CONCLUDING THE SALE

 OUTCOMES FROM THIS CHAPTER

- Learn how to close the sale
- Understand how to eliminate objections from your sales process
- Know how to price objections

COACHING SESSION 66

Self-assessment

Assessment criteria	Score
If a specific objection arises on a regular basis, I review my sales process and consider what I can do to avoid the objection arising.	
I ensure that I identify any potential objections during the discovery stage of my sales process and cover them in my sales proposal.	
I avoid being specific about costs until I am ready to present my proposal.	
I am aware of possible objections and have rehearsed my response to them.	
When negotiating, I always seek to understand things from my prospect's perspective so that I can create a win-win deal.	
TOTAL	

Score yourself between 1 and 5. A score of 5 means this statement is totally true; 1 means this statement is totally untrue. Total up your score. The maximum is 25 out of 25. Even if you give yourself a full score, I recommend you complete this chapter.

THE TRIAL CLOSE

Once you have delivered your compelling sales proposal, we need to start working towards getting a decision from our prospect. While we want to win the sale, we need a decision one way or another. In other words, we need to conclude the sale.

As your skill improves in negotiating the earlier stages in the consultative sales process, you will find that with many sales opportunities you will sail straight through the 'negotiate solution' stage without any change to your proposal. However, changes can still happen, especially where your sales opportunities have more than one person influencing the decision.

Once we have delivered our proposal, we need to find a way to proactively ask for the business. If we just deliver a proposal and wait for a response, we may find in many cases that we are waiting for a long time! We risk the prospects getting distracted with other things and the longer we leave it the bigger the risk that other events get in the way of the sale. This is often referred to as 'the long no.'

With consultative selling, you do not need to use any fancy or manipulative closing techniques. We can simply ask a question like:

- 'Would you like to go ahead?'

- 'Shall I book you in?'

- 'Do you have any questions or would you like me to organize the paperwork?'

In classic sales theory this is referred to as a 'trial close' because we ask the question to see how ready the prospect is to make a decision. The response we get will tell us how to proceed. When we ask our trial close question we could get a wide variety of responses but ultimately they will fall into one of four categories:

- Yes – meaning that they are happy with the proposed solution and would like to proceed.

- Yes, but – meaning that they are happy in principle but there is something they would like to change.

- No – meaning that they have decided not to proceed with your solution.

- No, but – they may be open to changing their mind if you are able to alter something.

'Yes' or 'No' are ideal because the prospect has made a clear decision. If we have done our work well, we will get more Yesses than Nos, on average. When we get a 'Yes, but' or a 'No, but' it means that the prospect has some kind of reservation that will require negotiation. Typical 'No, but' responses include:

- 'I want to have time to think about it.'

- 'I can't afford it at the moment.'

- 'I would like to look around.'

In sales, 'Yes, but' and 'No, but' responses are often referred to as an 'objection' and, in our consultative sales process, objections are managed as part of the 'negotiate solution' stage.

COACHING SESSION 67

In the space below, write one or more trial close questions you could use.

_____

_____

_____

REGULAR OBJECTIONS

The best way to manage objections is to avoid them arising in the first place. If you regularly get a particular objection, you should seek ways to pre-empt it in one or more of the following ways:

- Setting expectations in your marketing materials
- Changing your qualification criteria
- Handling the issue in your sales proposal

For example, if you regularly find out at the 'negotiate solution' stage of your sales process that the prospect cannot afford your solution, then it could be a problem with the way in which you are qualifying your sales opportunities or you may need to introduce some payment options.

Some salespeople pride themselves on being good on overcoming objections. However, in reality they just slow everything down and have the potential to cause friction and trust issues. Later in this chapter we will look at how to respond to objections but for now I would like you to consider objections you get regularly and what you could do to start eliminating them from your sales process.

Example

One customer I was working with was losing 25 per cent of their sales at the negotiating stage due to their payment terms. They required payment via direct debit and at the time there was a lot of bad coverage in the media about making payments by direct debit. Some experts were actively advising people not to give out bank details. The salespeople were getting prospects ready to buy but when they asked for information to complete the direct debit instructions, a significant proportion would change their mind.

When the salespeople started to ask for bank instructions instead of direct debit instructions, the drop-off rate shrunk to just 5 per cent. In other words, they won 20 per cent more sales just by changing two words!

♀♀ COACHING SESSION 68

List the objections you get on a regular basis and consider how you might pre-empt them in your sales process so that they arise less frequently.

Objections	How I can pre-empt them

RISK REDUCTION

Risk plays an important role in the decision-making process for buyers, even though it may not be on the top of their mind early in the sales process. When it comes down to deciding whether to go ahead with a proposal or deciding which supplier to choose, risk becomes more important, especially when committing to large expenditures or where the consequences of failure are high. Even though people in large companies are not spending their own money, they tend to play it safe because they are thinking of their career.

The good news is that if we can show our prospects that we are the safe option then they may be prepared to pay higher prices. This can be for a number of reasons, such as:

- They need to get it right first time.
- They do not want to have to pay twice to solve the problem.
- They don't want to waste time if it fails.
- The consequences of failure are high.
- They are worried about their job.

When it comes to selling services, there is often a perceived link between cost and quality. There is an assumption that if you charge high rates then you must be good at what you do. Conversely, when you are charging low rates there is an assumption that there is something wrong with what you do.

There is also a common assumption that a specialist is a lower-risk option than a generalist. If you needed legal advice, would you pay more for a specialist who has proven success in the area of concern or would you cut corners and go with the cheapest generalist you can find? People will pay more and they will find the money if they need to. Your job, when writing your proposal, is to convince the prospect that you are the 'safe pair of hands'. Unless your prospect is confident that you will be able to solve their problem and that you will not be wasting their time, you may even struggle to give away your solutions free!

When selling a similar product to your competitors, you can often justify higher prices with service-related features such as:

- reliability

- responsiveness

- industry experience

- local service

- global reach.

Obviously, these features need to be important to your target audience and they need to be things your competitors are not offering. For a global project, dealing with one company that has global reach is a lower-risk and more convenient option than having to deal with many suppliers in many countries and languages.

When there is no difference in your offering then there will always be pressure on price. In such cases, it may be easier to focus on a more specific target audience (see Chapter 2) than to come up with clever ways to overcome price objections.

Mitigating risks

Risk is something that is rarely spoken about but it is always there. We should proactively anticipate the risks that may be a concern to our prospects and seek ways to mitigate those risks.

Here are some examples of generic risks and some ideas for how you might seek to mitigate them.

Risk type	Possible mitigations
The problem will not be solved.	Emphasize your company's credentials. Give details of your methodology. Give some kind of guarantee. Give a case study and a customer reference.
The project will not finish on time.	Include an outline timeline. Include a guarantee. Give a customer reference.
The project will take up a lot of management time.	Include details of how you will manage the project and report progress.
The person allocated to the project will not be competent.	Include their name and bio.

⨀⨀ COACHING SESSION 69

Now identify specific risks that your customers may perceive with your products and services and ways you can mitigate those risks and reassure your prospects.

Risk	Mitigation

HANDLING OBJECTIONS

Assuming that you have updated your qualification process to remove any sales opportunities that are not a good fit, any objections you now get are likely to be about specific circumstances. Rather than fearing objections, if we anticipate them and decide how we will handle them then it becomes less of a challenge. Many salespeople find price the biggest challenge but if you have done your discovery well it should be fairly easy to handle.

The secret is to script out your responses to objections and then memorize and role play them so that you when you give your response it is done with confidence. Then, over time, you will naturally fine-tune your message.

One simple technique for finding the words is known as the 'Feel, Felt, Found' method:

- 'I know how you **Feel**' – You empathize with them.

- 'Many of our customers **Felt** that way' – You indicate that feeling that way is common.

- 'But what they **Found** is' – You tell them why it is not an issue.

This is just a framework and you can vary the words, although I recommend keeping the first line.

Examples

Objection	I can't afford your sales breakthrough session.
Response	I know how you feel.
	Most of my customers felt they could not afford to do the sales breakthrough at first ...
	But then they realized that the reason they couldn't afford it was very reason why they needed to do it, especially as I give a guarantee.
Comments	This is a much more elegant way of saying 'If you can't afford to then you can't afford not to...'
	The guarantee removes the risk of it not working for them.
	The third line changed the word 'found' to 'realized' as it's more appropriate.

Objection	I am looking for coaching on a face-to-face basis.
Response	I know how you feel.
	Many of my customers were just looking for face-to-face coaching.
	But after trying it, they found they actually *preferred* combining face-to-face coaching with telephone sessions. That's because it gave them more flexibility and made everything more affordable.
Comments	In this example, the second line replaces 'felt' with 'were looking for'.
	The third line emphasizes the benefits of combining face-to-face coaching with telephone-based coaching.

COACHING SESSION 70

Using the Feel, Felt, Found technique detailed above, script responses to your four most common objections.

1

Objection	
Response	

2

Objection	
Response	

3	
Objection	
Response	

4	
Objection	
Response	

FLUSHING OUT OBJECTIONS

In many cases, a prospect may not tell you they have an objection. It is more likely that they just do not respond to your proposal. Prior to you delivering your proposal, they will have been taking your calls and happy to speak to you. Then, once you have delivered your proposal, they disappear off the planet! Some people just do not like saying 'no' and others may want to think about it or go and speak to some other potential suppliers.

When your prospect stops talking to you then, in my experience, the best way to get the conversation started again is to take the position where you assume that they have decided not to proceed. Contact them on that basis and just ask for feedback. One of three things will happen:

- They tell you they are still interested.
- They tell you they are not interested and why.
- They tell you they are interested but have an issue with something.

It is best to get your prospects to make a decision even if that decision is 'No'.

NEGOTIATING PAST THE OBJECTION

Negotiation is a big subject and it is worth developing your negotiation skills if this is something you need to do regularly, especially if you need to negotiate with professional negotiators. However, here are some tips for negotiating your solution:

- Recognize that if they are negotiating, they are interested in doing business with you.
- Assume that your prospect has had training in negotiation.

- Never go into a negotiation without being prepared to say 'No'.
- Go into the negotiation seeking a win-win agreement.
- Decide on your ideal outcome for the negotiation and anticipate what you believe your prospect's outcome to be.
- Decide on your 'non-negotiables' and under what conditions you would be prepared to withdraw from the sale.
- Do not play games.
- Accept that your prospect may be playing games (e.g. 'Your prices are 30 per cent too high').
- Never give anything away without getting something in return (e.g. 'I can reduce the price if you are happy to pay in advance').
- Seek to change the scope rather than the price.
- Identify 'tradeables' which you can offer. Examples might be payment options or extra items that are of value to them but low cost to you (e.g. free subscription to your membership site worth £100).

COACHING SESSION 71

List some ideas of what you could offer or trade in your sales opportunities rather than reducing the price.

1. _____

_____

_____

_____

_____

_____

2. _____

_____

_____

_____

3.

4.

5.

NEXT STEPS

Now that we have looked at closing the sale, we need to look at the types of sales opportunities that are more complex and where more than one person is involved in the decision-making process.

TAKEAWAYS

What have I learned?

1. What is a trial close and why is it important?

_____

_____

_____

_____

_____

_____

_____

_____

_____

2. What is the best way to deal with objections?

_____

_____

_____

_____

_____

_____

_____

_____

_____

3. In the context of a negotiation, what are tradeables and why are they important?

12 | HANDLING COMPLEX SALES OPPORTUNITIES

✔ OUTCOMES FROM THIS CHAPTER

- Handle sales with a complex decision-making process
- Know how to assess who has the most influence over the decision
- Understand the importance of finding supporters

🗣🗣 COACHING SESSION 72

Self-assessment

Assessment criteria	Score
I always seek to understand how a decision will be made.	
I always seek a supporter to provide me with background information about people with influence on the decision.	
I spend most of my discovery time with people who have the most influence on the decision.	
I seek to understand the personal motivation for change of the people who have most influence on the decision.	
I ensure that my proposal addresses the needs and motivations of the people who have most influence on the decision.	
TOTAL	

Score yourself between 1 and 5. A score of 5 means this statement is totally true; 1 means this statement is totally untrue. Total up your score. The maximum is 25 out of 25. Even if you give yourself a full score, I recommend you complete this chapter.

WHO IS THE DECISION MAKER?

As we discovered in Chapter 7, people within a prospect's organization often think they are the decision maker even if they are not the person who ultimately signs the cheque. Indeed, in larger organizations you could get the situation where several people believe they are the decision maker and, in some respects, they are.

The issue is that, in the real world, decisions are not always made by one single person. Things can get more complex. The owner of a small company may turn to a special adviser to select and manage a supplier. Even though the adviser will not be the person signing the cheques, refusing to deal with the adviser is a quick way to be ruled out. This is especially true if the adviser is the person you will have to deal with after the deal is done.

In larger organizations, we may have several people who will have an influence on the final decision and if we do not include them in our discovery process we run the risk that they will use their influence in favour of a competitor.

An extreme example of a complex sale is where a committee will make a final decision by discussion and voting. Some law firms still operate in this way. In such circumstances we need to know who particular committee members will listen to.

In short, we need to take time to understand how decisions are to be made and who will be involved in making the decision, so that we can influence the influencers.

There will almost always be one person who is the ultimate decision maker even though this may change depending on what is being purchased. The ultimate decision maker may not have the most influence over the final decision but they do have the ability to override any decision that has been made. They can say 'yes' even though the influencers have said 'no' and they can say 'no' even though the key influencers have said 'yes'.

For some types of purchase, the budget holder may be the ultimate decision maker. In other types of purchase, they could have a budget but, because of the type of expenditure, they need approval for the budget to be released. The bottom line is that we need to discover who is the ultimate decision maker and who else is highly influential in deciding what to buy and who to buy it from.

Decision influencers could include:

- project managers
- internal and external consultants
- people who will be affected by the project
- financial specialists
- professional buyers
- legal advisers.

When we are pursuing a sales opportunity, especially if it is with a large organization, we should be discovering who has the influence on the final decision and developing relationships with them. The way we do this is by doing a sales opportunity map.

Example

Name	Job	Relationship	Influence on decision	Comments
Cathy Greggs	Chief Executive	Low	Medium	Ultimate decision maker
???	Marketing Director	None	High	
Janice Evans	Marketing Manager	High	Low	
Sally Woodstock	Sales Director	High	High	

In this example sales opportunity map, we can see that the two people with the most influence on the ultimate decision are the Sales and Marketing Directors. There is an excellent relationship with the Sales Director but is it enough to win the sale? The Marketing Director may have a relationship with a major competitor that provides a persuasive case for why they should win the contract. A salesperson in this scenario might seek to gain insights about the Marketing Manager and work on developing that relationship. In this example, the majority of the discovery stage would probably be spent with the Sales and Marketing Directors rather than the ultimate decision maker.

As you can see in the above example, we do not even know the Marketing Director's name at the moment. An action from doing the sales opportunity map could be to find out the name from Janice Evans and as much background information as we can. Even though Janice is not influential in the decision, she can still be a useful source of information.

⟨⟩ COACHING SESSION 73

For one of your current sales opportunities, map out the people who have an influence on the ultimate decision.

Name	Job	Relationship	Influence on decision	Comments

MOTIVATION TO CHANGE

Even though you may have an excellent relationship with someone who is highly influential on the ultimate decision, you may still not win the sale if there is insufficient personal motivation to change.

For example, you are selling an accounting software package to a company. The Finance Director is the ultimate decision maker and will look to the Finance Manager for guidance. You have an excellent relationship with the Finance Manager but he likes their existing accounting software package and does not see the need for change. The Finance Director is unlikely to go against the Finance Manager's wishes and, unless you are able to help the Finance Manager 'find' a compelling reason for change, the sales opportunity is unlikely to go anywhere.

Personal motives could be related to the job, such as being able to produce reports more quickly. They could, however, be nothing to do with the job. In the above example, let's assume you discover that the Finance Manager is ambitious and looking to move to another company at some point. They may think differently about your software package if they knew that it was the market leader and the one they are most likely to be using if they were to move to another company. Having experience with the 'industry standard' accounting software package may improve their job-hunting prospects.

🗩🗩 COACHING SESSION 74

Using the information from coaching session 73, now add some extra information. Grade their motivation to change as high, medium, or low and write in their personal motive if you know it. If you do not then find a way of discovering what it is.

Name	Job	Relationship	Influence on decision	Motivation to change	Personal motive

GENERATING ACTION

The ultimate purpose of a sales opportunity map is to generate action. Each time you map out the sales opportunity, things become clearer and the sales opportunity will have progressed further. For example, when mapping out a sales opportunity, if you identify that you do not know who the ultimate decision maker is then you then create an action to find out. If you see that you have a poor relationship with someone who has a lot of influence then you create an action to work on the relationship. Many of the actions will be around booking discovery meetings with key influencers so that you can apply the GRIN model to their circumstances and discover not only what they want but why they want it.

If all your sales opportunities are complex, I recommend you read *The New Strategic Selling* by Robert B. Miller and Stephen E. Heiman. Their system is comprehensive and widely used by major corporations. They call their sales opportunity maps 'Blue Sheets', because they are coloured blue. A blue sheet brings lots of information about the sales opportunity together into one place. One of the things I especially like about the strategic selling approach to sales opportunity mapping is the concept of red flags. Their blue sheets are designed to be used where there are teams of people working on a sales opportunity. The blue sheet is printed and where anything needs to be highlighted you mark the sheet with a red flag. Red flags then indicate that action is required.

The 'blue sheet' system is very good when you have large teams all working on a big opportunity. For example, if you are selling software and you need to get pre-sales and post-sales consultants involved in the sale then the physical blue sheet is a great reference point and focus of attention. The danger of consigning sales opportunity maps to spreadsheets is that, over time, the focus of attention shifts from driving action to the mechanics of filling in the spreadsheet.

With smaller opportunities, rather than have a form, I just write out the headings on a whiteboard or piece of A3 paper. I find that part of the clarity comes through writing the sales opportunity map out, even though this may seem like an inefficient approach.

However you decide to do your sales opportunity maps and whatever extra information you add, please remember that the purpose is to gain clarity and drive the action required to win the sale. An output of doing a sales opportunity map should be to create an action list which you subsequently track to ensure that the actions get done!

COACHING SESSION 75

From your sales opportunity map in coaching session 73, list the actions you need to take to move your sales opportunity forward.

1. _____

_____

_____

2. _____

_____

_____

3. _____

_____

_____

4. _____

_____

_____

5. _____

_____

_____

FINDING SUPPORTERS

If you are wondering where the name 'sales opportunity map' comes from, there are a lot of similarities with a conventional road map. If we want to travel to a place we do not know very well, we consult a map. Sometimes the route we intend to take is blocked and provided the map has enough detail we should be able to find alternative routes to our destination.

Discovering the detail to complete a sales opportunity map can be made significantly easier by finding people who can help you with that information. These might often be people you are friendly with who work within the same organization and who want to see you succeed but do not have an influence on the decision.

In the above example, Janice Evans, the Marketing Manager, has a low influence on the decision but the relationship with Janice is high. Meeting up with Janice over a cup of coffee may be all that is required to get her input on how the decision will really be made, despite what you have been told, and background information about each person.

Some companies use the term 'mole' instead of supporter. This is because it can seem as if you have someone on the inside passing you information. I prefer to think of it as having someone on your side who wants your solution but who does not have the direct influence to make it happen. You do need to take care in selecting your supporter as there is the risk that your supporter is actually supporting a competitor and passing you false information or using the relationship to pass information to a competitor. Personally I have not had that happen, but just be clear about the motives of your supporters as much as anyone else involved in the sales opportunity.

When you map out a sales opportunity for the first time, one of your first actions might be to find a supporter. Indeed, you may want to find more than one supporter. The more input you can gain the better. You may have different supporters in different parts of the same organization. After all, with large sales opportunities, it is likely that few people have the complete picture. Sometimes personal assistants make great supporters, which is why, referring back to the chapter on cold calling, it is good to work with them rather than considering them the enemy!

♀♀ COACHING SESSION 76

In the sales opportunity you have been working on in this chapter, list some potential supporters and actions you can take to develop the relationship and get them onside.

Potential supporter	Action to get them onside

FORMAL BIDS

Another thing that makes sales opportunities more complex is where you are part of a formal bidding process. Although everything is this book is relevant, there are some additional considerations to bear in mind.

It can be tempting to chase after large contracts, especially where the requirements are clearly laid out. In our consultative sales process, getting a request for proposal (RFP) or an invitation to tender (ITT) gets you to the 'generate interest' stage. You still need to take the sales opportunity through each stage of your sales process. The main difference is that the bid document may specify how the proposal needs to be presented. In Chapter 10 we looked at proposals and you need to include the various pieces of information into the bid document even though the headings may differ from your normal proposals.

The thing to watch for in these bids is that they are often issued to benchmark their existing supplier against the market to ensure that they keep their prices as low as possible. When going through the 'qualify interest' stage, you need to establish whether there is an existing supplier, why they are inviting bids and whether the existing supplier is being allowed to bid. Unless there is a compelling reason to change suppliers, the chances are that the prospect will not. The company will either satisfy themselves that the rate they are paying is reasonable or get their incumbent supplier to adjust their prices which, in most cases, is what happens.

The other trap to watch out for is where one of your competitors has been involved in the creation of the RFT or ITT bid documents. Sometimes the bid process is a formality and the prospect has already decided who they are going to work with and that company helped them to create the bid document. Again, as part of your qualifying criteria you should look at whether competitors have an existing relationship. Ideally, you will review the likelihood of winning a bid before investing time and money in competing. Many companies do not bother bidding unless they are a large brand or have an established relationship with someone on the inside who has influence on the outcome.

→ NEXT STEPS

This is the end of Part 2, on closing the sale. Part 3 focuses on increasing your productivity and the next chapter is all about creating and achieving motivational goals.

TAKEAWAYS

What have I learned?

1. What is a complex sale?

_____

_____

_____

_____

_____

_____

_____

_____

_____

_____

2. What is a sales opportunity map and why would you use one?

_____

_____

_____

_____

_____

_____

_____

_____

_____

_____

3. Under what circumstances might a budget holder not be the ultimate decision maker?

_____

_____

_____

_____

_____

_____

_____

_____

_____

_____

_____

_____

_____

_____

_____

_____

_____

_____

_____

_____

_____

_____

PART 3
IMPROVING SALES EFFECTIVENESS

13 YOUR MOTIVE FOR ACTION

✔ OUTCOMES FROM THIS CHAPTER

- Create motivational goals that will increase your sales activity
- Learn how to make your goals more compelling
- Understand the importance of having a plan to achieve your goals

COACHING SESSION 77

Self-assessment

Assessment criteria	Score
I have written personal goals that keep me motivated.	
My goals inspire me to take action.	
I regularly visualize achieving my goals.	
I have a plan for achieving my goals.	
I have monthly sales targets that I have aligned to my personal goals.	
TOTAL	

Score yourself between 1 and 5. A score of 5 means this statement is totally true; 1 means this statement is totally untrue. Total up your score. The maximum is 25 out of 25. Even if you give yourself a full score, I recommend you complete this chapter.

SELLING IS AN ACTIVITY GAME

It is often said that 'sales is a numbers game'. I prefer to think of sales as an activity game. We can have highly polished selling skills and yet, without enough activity in the right places, we will not sell much. I have seen people fairly new to sales outsell people with years of experience just because they take on more activity. Obviously, we will achieve more if we have the skill *and* the action but sometimes people become obsessed with developing their skills without doing enough activity to be able to develop the skills.

Our self-motivation drives our activity levels and if we want to increase activity then we first need to increase our motive for action. However, we need to move our understanding of motivation beyond the sense of feeling motivated. While it is good to feel motivated, our self-motivation needs to run much deeper than just the feeling. You may not necessarily *feel* motivated all the time but you will do the activity anyway because your goals are important to you and you are committed to achieving your goals. It's a bit like an athlete who has a goal to compete in the Olympic Games. The athlete may not feel like getting up and going for a run early in the morning when it is cold and icy outside. They do it because they remember why they are doing it and that the training will help them achieve their goal.

You can achieve both the deep motivation and the feeling of motivation by focusing your goals on those areas of your personal life that are most important to you.

Example

Rank	Area of life	Why it is important
1.	Family and friends	Because I love my family and enjoy spending time with them and also with my friends
2.	Finances	Because I want to provide financial stability and security for my family and be able to afford to do fun things with my family and friends
3.	Health	Because I want to stay healthy and set a good example for my children

In this particular example you can see that there is a common theme but this is not essential. Having goals that are focused on these areas will be more motivational for the individual than goals set out of context.

COACHING SESSION 78

Using a sheet of paper, make a list of the areas of your life that are most important to you. Keep going until you cannot think of any more. Then select the top three.

Rank	Area of life	Why it is important
1.		
2.		
3.		

CREATING GOALS WITH EMOTIONAL PULL

Motivation can be either positive or negative. We talk about using 'the carrot or the stick' when motivating others. Carrot motivation works on the anticipation of future pleasure. The stick, on the other hand, works on avoiding pain. Some people tend to focus on what they want (pleasure), whereas others are more focused on avoiding what they don't want (pain).

There is a problem with goals driven by pain motivation in that we tend to put our focus on the source of the pain rather than on what we want instead. For example, John hates his job. He is underpaid, under-appreciated and does not get on with his colleagues. The situation is causing him distress (pain) and it is motivating him to find another job. At this point there is the danger than John accepts the first new job that comes along (to remove the source of pain), rather than being focusing on the kind of job that will both remove the pain and give him pleasure.

Goal achievement is something the human brain does well. We tend to achieve what we focus on. Unfortunately, our brains have a limit when it comes to focus and so when we are focusing on what we don't want, we are effectively giving incorrect instructions to the goal achievement part of our brain. It is a little bit like typing the wrong address into a satellite navigation system. Focusing on what we do want will increase our levels of achievement and it also feels better to be motivated by pleasure rather than driven by negative emotions.

Before we start to work on your goals, I would just like you to look at the areas of your life you identified as being most important to you, and consider some of the things you don't want and then consider what you would like instead.

Example

What I don't want	What I would like instead
I don't want my children to have a bad education.	I want to be able to afford to fund my children's education.
I don't want to be in debt.	I want to pay off all my debts.
I don't want to be poor in retirement.	I want to have sufficient savings so that I can maintain our current lifestyle when I retire.

Thinking about the top three important areas of your life, first list some of the things you don't want and then for each one consider what you would like instead.

What I don't want	What I would like instead

CREATING WELL-FORMED GOALS

To take advantage of our brain's goal achievement functionality, there are some important qualities each of our goals should have:

Clarity

Many people have goals that are very vague. We need goals so clear that we can envision them. I will show you how to envision your goals later in this chapter but for now just be clear what specifically you want and when you want it by. For example, rather than having a goal to earn more money, you should be specific about what you want to be earning and by when.

Achievability

Although, at this stage, it is not important to know *how* you will achieve a goal, it is critical that you believe your goal can be achieved somehow. Achievability is often influenced by timescales. For example, it may be totally achievable to double your current income in two years' time but less achievable in three months' time. Again, if you do not, deep down, believe the goal is achievable then it's better to change the timescale rather than abandon the goal.

Testability

You need to have some kind of test to know when you have achieved your goal. A goal to live in a particular type of house by a particular date is easy to test. We are either living in that type of house or not, and until we are we have not achieved our goal. A goal relating to something less tangible like a level of skill or confidence can be tested through self-assessment. Using a scale of 1 to 10, you assess your current level and then in your goal you specify your desired level. For example, someone with a goal to feel more confident with cold calling would ask himself:

'On a scale of 1 to 10 (10 being totally confident), how confident do I feel right now?'

Let's say that the answer was 2 out of 10. The person can now set a goal to reach a confidence level of 7 out of 10 within six months. In six months' time they simply need to ask themselves the same self-assessment question to test whether they have achieved their goal or not.

The WOW! factor

While all your goals will be important to you, I want you to be able to pay attention to the goals that have real emotional pull. We want goals that are going to get you so excited about achieving them that they will drive your sales activity, especially on a day when things are not going according to plan. The WOW! factor scores are high, medium or low. High means that it gets you really excited just thinking about it. Low means that it does not really have any impact. Medium is just moderately exciting.

Price

The price of achieving your goal will be a combination of time and money. We should be aware of how much time and effort our goals will require so that collectively they become realistic. We may need to review timescales of specific goals so that they collectively become more achievable. While it is important to research the cost and effort of your goals, for now just use a score of high, medium or low.

Having goals that have a high WOW! factor and a low price can provide the short-term motivation to drive the achievement of longer-term goals.

👥 COACHING SESSION 80

Using the results of the previous coaching session, turn them into goals. Feel free to add more goals too.

What you want	When you want it by	WOW! factor	Price

BRINGING YOUR GOALS TO LIFE

When we begin to envision our goals, they start to become real and we begin to activate our brain's goal achievement functionality. Sometimes referred to as visualization, envisioning is about imagining what it would be like once you have achieved your goal. The goal achievement of your brain then starts helping you towards its achievement. You will begin noticing things that you may not have noticed before and you will be motivated to do things even if you do not feel like it. Visualization is now commonplace within all kinds of sports, from tennis to motor racing.

We are now going to take one of your goals and start to imagine what it will be like once you have achieved your goal. We need to be imagining it as if it is virtual-reality movie involving all your five senses:

- Sight – What do you see through your own eyes as you look around?
- Sound – What do you hear?
- Feeling – What can you feel?
- Taste – What can you taste?
- Smell – What can you smell?

Using the example of a goal to win an Olympic gold medal, we will go through each of the five senses one by one.

What can you see?

I am in the Olympic stadium and, looking around, I can see it is completely full. I can see the other medal winners next to me. We are all standing on the podium and I am on the spot for the winner. In front of me, I can see my name in lights. I then see a posy of flowers being handed to me and then shortly after that I see the gold medal being put over my head and as I wave to the people in the stadium I see everyone cheering and waving flags.

What can you hear?

I hear the roar of the crowd, which suddenly goes silent as the national anthems are played, followed by a massive roar afterwards. I hear my name on the public-address system and as the medal is placed over my head I am congratulated by the dignitaries and I am saying to myself: 'I did it!'

What can you feel?

It's a lovely sunny day and I can feel the warmth of the sun on my face mixed with a soft breeze. I can feel the podium beneath my feet as I step on to it and I can feel the posy of flowers in my hand and then an elated feeling when the gold medal is placed over my head and I wave to the crowd. I feel a sense of pride as my country's national anthem is playing and I feel the weight of the medal as it hangs around my neck.

What can you taste?

I had a cold drink immediately before the ceremony and I can still taste it.

What can you smell?

I can smell the perfume of the dignitary as she places the gold medal over my head.

Notes

You will notice that the example above is in the present tense and in the first person. This makes it easier to imagine. You just imagine you are actually there. Whether or not you can actually visualize the scene in your 'mind's eye' is not important. What is important is that you start to experience what it will be like. You may find that changing some of the details will make it more motivational. For example, the gold medal winner imagining family members hugging them afterwards could be the one detail that makes the whole vision significantly more motivational.

Some people find it easier to imagine something once they have added the sound or the feelings. With the sounds, you have both external sounds and also internal dialogue that you may be saying to yourself. Similarly, with the feelings, you have what you can touch and feel as well as emotions. The sense of taste and smell can really help but sometimes you may need to be creative. Including something like a glass of champagne or a cup of coffee in your celebrations can add both taste and smell, together with additional feelings. You can imagine holding the glass and the sensation as you take a drink.

👥 COACHING SESSION 81

Using one of your goals from the previous coaching session and following the example, write out each of the five senses of your virtual reality movie.

Goal:	
What do I see?	
What do I hear?	
What do I feel?	
What do I taste?	
What do I smell?	

MAKING PLANS

A goal without a plan is just a wish. We need to take action towards achieving our goal and this is where we should be dovetailing our personal goals in with our sales activity. How much more will you have to sell in order to achieve your goal? If your situation means that you do not directly increase earnings through increased sales then you should be clear how achieving increased sales will help you achieve your goals. For example, you may be able to negotiate a higher salary based on achieving sales targets. Whether your goals require you to achieve sales targets or not, it is still important to have a plan for their achievement. However, if you want to increase your sales then it works best where achieving your goals is linked in some way to your reaching your sales targets. For example, you could use some of your WOW! goals as a reward for achieving particular sales targets.

 **NEXT STEPS**

Having motivational goals, combined with sales targets, will help to drive forward your activity. In the next chapter we will be looking at things that can work against our motivation and diminish our performance.

 **TAKEAWAYS**

What have I learned?

1. Why is it important to make your goals specific to certain areas of your life?

_____

_____

_____

_____

_____

_____

_____

_____

_____

_____

2. Why is it important to have clear goals?

_____

_____

_____

_____

_____

_____

_____

_____

_____

_____

3. What is visualization and how does it help make goals more motivational?

_____

_____

_____

_____

_____

_____

_____

_____

_____

_____

_____

_____

_____

_____

_____

_____

_____

_____

_____

_____

_____

_____

14 MANAGING YOUR EMOTIONS

OUTCOMES FROM THIS CHAPTER

- Understand the importance of managing your emotional state
- Learn three ways to change your emotional state
- Learn how to boost confidence for meetings and presentations

COACHING SESSION 82

Self-assessment

Assessment criteria	Score
I am aware of my emotional state when working with customers.	
I manage my emotions when I need to.	
I am conscious of my posture and breathing.	
I prepare myself mentally for sales meetings and presentations.	
I have rituals that I can follow to get me into the state I need for top performance.	
TOTAL	

Score yourself between 1 and 5. A score of 5 means this statement is totally true; 1 means this statement is totally untrue. Total up your score. The maximum is 25 out of 25. Even if you give yourself a full score, I recommend you complete this chapter.

THE IMPORTANCE OF MANAGING YOUR EMOTIONS

The way we feel can have a big impact on our sales activity. If we are feeling nervous and lacking in confidence, besides being unpleasant, it could be misinterpreted by a prospective customer as a lack confidence in our products and services. Negative emotions can sap our energy and the anticipation of negative feelings may even put us off doing any sales activity at all. Even though we may be highly motivated, we can still be affected by negative emotions and we need to know how to deal with this so that our sales performance does not suffer.

Imagine you have a sales meeting with an ideal prospective customer and then, ten minutes before the meeting is due to start, you discover that a major customer has decided to switch to a competitor's product which will upset your sales targets quite severely. The risk is that this situation negatively affects your performance in your important sales meeting, if not for the rest of the day. In sales, things like this happen and the more sales activity we do, the more knock-backs we will get. If we want to take our sales performance to a higher level, we need to learn how to deal with these inevitable knock-backs.

The thing to realize about emotions is that they are simply chemicals released by our brain in response to a situation. Your brain is deciding how you should feel and then causing your body to have that sensation. It is part of the primitive part of our brain which kept us alive when we were all living in caves! The impact of these chemicals will wear off over time and can be quickly replaced with other chemicals that feel much better.

Many people are unaware that we can exert some control over our emotions and stop the negative emotions affecting our performance. To do this we need to become aware of the circumstances that trigger a change in our emotional state. It could be anything from the way someone looks at us, the way they speak to us, specific words they use and even particular events that happen. From the moment we are born our brains are busy learning to distinguish between danger and pleasure, and releasing chemicals to control our emotional states. There will always be a cue that triggers the emotion and the first step towards controlling our emotional state is to become aware of these emotional triggers.

COACHING SESSION 83

Keep a diary for a couple of days, noticing anything that changes your emotional state, either positively or negatively. Pay attention to what triggered the change in emotion. Also make a note of important details associated with the emotion such as where in the body you experience the emotion, any movement in the body, your posture and breathing, etc.

Date	Time	Emotional state	Trigger	Details

POSTURE, BREATHING AND MOTION

If you were to look at a depressed person from a distance, you could probably tell that they were depressed just by observing their posture and the way in which they were breathing. Likewise, if you were to look at a highly motivated person from a distance, you would also be able to tell their emotional state from their posture and breathing. The way we feel has an impact on our posture and breathing. The reverse is also true. Our posture and breathing can have an impact on how we feel – either negatively or positively. We can take advantage of this phenomenon to help us get into an empowering emotional state when we really need it.

A good example of using posture and breathing to change your emotional state would be when making cold calls. Many people claim they feel a lot more relaxed about cold calling when they are standing and moving about rather than sitting.

Do this little experiment right now, if you can. If you are sitting then stand up. Straighten your back and take three deep breaths from your stomach while putting on a big smile. Make sure you smile with your eyes too. Just by smiling, even though it is a fake smile, you will begin to feel better. Standing and taking deep breaths should help you relax and – when combined with the smile – will help you feel more positive.

From a physical point of view, we tend to breathe much better when we are standing; and breathing from the stomach tends to be very relaxing. The way we move is an aspect of posture and standing and moving in the way you would when feeling confident can help to boost confidence.

Now that you are becoming more aware of your emotional states, the next step is also to become aware of things like your posture, breathing and motion while you are in those emotional states. Noticing them when in a negative state can become a spur for us to change our posture, breathing and motion; and noticing them when feeling in an empowering state will help us know what to change our posture, breathing and motion to.

COACHING SESSION 84

For two days, pay attention to your emotional states. If you experience any significant positive or negative emotions, pay attention to your posture, breathing and motion and make notes about them here. See how you can alter your emotional state by changing your posture, breathing and motion to that of a more empowering emotional state.

Emotional state	Posture	Breathing	Motion

MENTAL REHEARSAL

Fear and anxiety are a common issue in sales, especially when it comes to important meetings. A powerful technique that will give you a real boost to your confidence is called 'mental rehearsal'. Mental rehearsal is used widely by sportspeople to improve their performance and it literally means rehearsing in your mind. You build up a mental movie of how you want the meeting to go and you visualize the movie. Rather than imagining the meeting going badly and feeling anxious about it, you will be imagining the meeting going well and feeling confident about it.

Mental rehearsal works in a similar way to the flight simulators that airline pilots use to train with. It seems that the human brain is unable to tell the difference between something experienced and something vividly imagined. Just as pilots use flight simulators to practise responding to difficult circumstances, we are using mental rehearsal to simulate key aspects of the meeting. Each time we mentally rehearse something, we are giving ourselves the equivalent of a real-life experience.

Mental rehearsal can be used to develop selling skills and I have personally found it effective in improving interpersonal skills such as the ability to read body language and networking. I was first introduced to it, however, when struggling to overcome nerves before important sales meetings.

The more we mentally rehearse having relaxed and confident meetings, the more we condition ourselves to have relaxed and confident meetings and the better the meetings tend to go. By the time we have the meeting, we are mentally prepared. Mental rehearsal works, no matter how fast or slowly we play the movie in our mind's eye. You do not have to be able to 'see' the mental movie in your mind's eye for the technique to work.

You can do mental rehearsal at any time but I find it particularly effective as a confidence booster when I do it shortly before a meeting. For example, if driving by car, arrive ten minutes earlier than normal and do the mental rehearsal in the car before you go in. If travelling by public transport, you can do it there.

You do need to create the movie in a particular way: it needs to be like a virtual-reality movie where you imagine things as if you are there, looking through your own eyes, in a similar way to how we envisioned our goals in Chapter 13.

Step 1: Create three mini-movies

Your first mini-movie should be of when you first meet your prospective customer. You have an instant rapport – it seems as if you have known the person a long time even though you have never met before. You give a firm handshake and make good eye contact. You feel confident and connected as you lead the small talk.

Your second mini-movie should relate to the meeting itself. You are asking some great questions and getting lots of useful information back. You are feeling calm and confident. Your prospective customer is doing most of the talking and you are listening intently and making notes, where appropriate. You can tell that there is good rapport between all the people in the room.

Your third mini-movie should begin at the end of the meeting, where you are shaking hands. You know the meeting has gone well and everyone is relaxed. There is plenty of rapport and you are feeling confident and elated.

Step 2: Play the three movies from beginning to end

Now play the mini-movies in your mind, one after another, starting with the initial meeting and finishing with the end of the meeting. Play the three movies over and over again in your mind, getting faster and faster each time until it is just a blur. You should now be ready to do your meeting in total confidence!

🗩🗩 COACHING SESSION 85

For your next sales meeting, use the mental rehearsal technique prior to the meeting.

BOOSTING CONFIDENCE FOR SALES PRESENTATIONS

Some people are confident in sales meetings but get racked with nerves when they need to give a formal presentation. The mental rehearsal technique is very effective for boosting confidence in making presentations too. If it is just a short presentation, you would do the same thing and create a series of three virtual-reality mental movies – but this time starting at the end when you are getting your applause, then visualizing the middle where you are delivering your presentation confidently and people are listening with interest and laughing in the right places, and finally the beginning when you start strongly and confidently.

There is no reason to limit the number of mini-movies to three. You can add as many additional movies as you need. Indeed, I have developed an advanced form of the mental rehearsal technique detailed above for delivering formal presentations, so that I am not only confident but also engaging and able to speak effectively without having to refer to notes. I call this the 'Mary Poppins' technique.

In the movie *Mary Poppins*, the character played by Dick Van Dyke is called Bert. At one point in the movie Bert is outside a park with a number of chalk paintings on the pavement and Bert, Mary Poppins and the two children she is looking after jump into the painting and the picture becomes real. With the Mary Poppins technique you lay out your slides on the floor and go through them one by one, doing a mental rehearsal for each slide. Even if I do not intend using slides in my presentation, I will still create slides for the purpose of doing the Mary Poppins technique.

Step 1: Prepare your presentation

You should wait until you are happy with your presentation before using the Mary Poppins technique. I recommend you practise delivering your presentation a couple of time before doing the Mary Poppins technique, to ensure that you have the flow of the presentation right and also for the timings. If you have a specific time allocated then you can write out your presentation. As a general rule, 150 words will equate to a minute of presentation, so if you have been given ten minutes you should make sure your presentation is less than 1,500 words, especially if you want to leave time for questions.

Step 2: Lay out your slides on the floor

Create the slides for your presentation, making sure you have a slide for the opening and closing of your presentation. Print out the slides, one slide to a page, and lay them out in a straight line, in the correct order. You will be using these slides like stepping stones, so they will need to be one pace apart.

Step 3: Mentally rehearse each slide

Starting with the very first slide, stand on the slide printout on the floor and mentally rehearse that part of your presentation. You do not have to mentally rehearse delivering your speech word for word; you would do that in the same way as part of your normal preparation. Here we are mentally rehearsing the delivery of your presentation and the audience reaction. Imagine yourself feeling confident, moving purposefully, and the audience reaction to your delivery. As you step on each slide on the floor, just say out loud a word or phrase that sums up that slide before doing the mental rehearsal for that slide. Then when you have completed that slide, you step on to the next slide and repeat the process. You keep doing this until you have mentally rehearsed all the slides in your presentation.

Step 4: Repeat the process

Once you have completed the whole presentation and you are standing on the last slide, you should then walk around to the first slide and do it all over again. It is important that you do this immediately rather than repeating the process another time.

Now walk back to the beginning and repeat the process again but this time you can just say the word or phrase you associated with the slide. Do this a further two times, stepping quite quickly through all the slides from beginning to end.

COACHING SESSION 86

For your next presentation, use the Mary Poppins technique as part of your preparation. Write down some notes here.

1. _____

2. _____

3. _____

4. _____

5. _____

6. _____

7. _____

NEXT STEPS

Now that we have learned how to get motivated and manage our emotions, the next thing we will look at is how to develop the right mindset for sales success.

 **TAKEAWAYS**

What have I learned?

1. Why is it important in sales to manage your emotions?

_____

_____

_____

_____

_____

_____

_____

_____

_____

2. What impact do posture, breathing and motion have on our emotional state?

_____

_____

_____

_____

_____

_____

_____

_____

_____

3. What is mental rehearsal and how would you use it to prepare for an important meeting?

_____

_____

_____

_____

_____

_____

_____

_____

_____

_____

_____

_____

_____

_____

_____

_____

_____

_____

_____

_____

_____

_____

_____

_____

15 DEVELOPING A MINDSET FOR SALES SUCCESS

 OUTCOMES FROM THIS CHAPTER

- Understand the importance of mindset in sales
- Know how assumptions and beliefs can impact sales performance
- Know how affirmations can help improve your sales performance

COACHING SESSION 87

Self-assessment

Assessment criteria	Score
I work on developing the right mindset for sales.	
I have a sales mentor who is at the level of sales performance I am aiming for.	
I always challenge my assumptions, especially if they could affect my sales results.	
I seek to convert my limiting beliefs into something more empowering.	
I use affirmations to help develop my sales mindset.	
TOTAL	

Score yourself between 1 and 5. A score of 5 means this statement is totally true; 1 means this statement is totally untrue. Total up your score. The maximum is 25 out of 25. Even if you give yourself a full score, I recommend you complete this chapter.

WORKING ON YOUR MINDSET

In sports, the difference between the top performers and the average performers often comes down to their mindset. You sometimes get the phenomenon of sportspeople who perform excellently in training but when it comes to competing they fail to recreate the same levels of performance. The same is true in sales. We can get reasonable sales results just through technique and activity alone. However, even someone with a natural flair for sales, the so-called 'born salesperson', will need to work on their mindset if they want to go from being a gifted amateur to becoming a professional.

Many people have some mixed-up thinking about sales, salespeople and what selling is about. Some of this thinking can have a negative impact on sales performance and even cause negative emotions. It is a little like running a marathon with a sack of rocks on your back. You can still do it but it will probably be a little uncomfortable and take a lot more effort.

Personal development had a massive impact on my progress in sales and it will be the same for you. It is no surprise that the biggest readers of sales books are the ones who least need it. They know that small differences in their thinking can make a big difference in their sales results. I was taught by a mentor to read for 15 minutes a day. Over the course of a year that equates to 90 hours of learning. Twenty years later I still continue the habit because it has become enjoyable and pays very well!

Mindset also includes attitude, which is beyond the scope of this book but can have an impact on sales performance, especially where the individual has a negative attitude towards things like other people, their product or the customers. When coaching people who have a negative attitude, I normally find that getting them focused on their goals and building their self-motivation helps to improve their attitude. Reading and personal development then helps to reinforce the attitude. For some of my book recommendations, please visit the references section of this book.

FINDING A MENTOR

One very useful way of helping you to adopt the mindset of a top-performing salesperson is to be mentored by one. It is certainly one of the areas that particularly made, and continues to make, a difference for me in my personal development journey. A mentor does not need to cost anything, apart from time, as many people enjoy mentoring others because it helps them to better understand what they do well and there is the satisfaction of helping someone else. People who have benefited from free mentoring often then pass on the favour to someone else.

Mentoring is different from coaching since its purpose is to learn how to think in the right way.

My first mentor worked in the same organization as me and allowed me to sit in on sales meetings with him and observe and then ask questions afterwards. I was always asking 'why?' questions. I wanted to know why he did certain things differently from me or how I would have done them. Knowing why certain things are important helps to change our mindset, especially if we are learning from people we trust and respect.

Eventually my mentor would sit in on some of my sales meetings and afterwards provided encouragement and pointed out where I could make improvements. He would also review my proposals and give me positive feedback.

Your choice of mentor is important. While it could be your boss, it does not have to be. There does need to be a good, honest and open relationship between you and you need to feel comfortable following the advice of the other person. It is better to get someone in your own line of sales and at the level of performance you are aiming for rather than just someone you believe to be good at sales.

COACHING SESSION 88

Create a shortlist of people you would like to have as a mentor and how you will go about asking them.

1. _____

_____

2. _____

_____

3. _____

_____

4. _____

_____

5. _____

_____

6. _____

_____

ASSUMPTIONS

As humans, we are good at making assumptions. We seem comfortable about accepting that certain things are true without requiring proof. For example, we may incorrectly assume that some who expresses an interest in our products and services is actually interested in buying from us. On the other hand, we may incorrectly assume, during a discovery meeting, that a prospect is not interested because they did not talk much. In these types of situations it pays to be aware of our assumptions and test them to avoid wasting time or walking away from a golden opportunity.

Here are some other common assumptions in sales:

- Your prospects are telling the truth.
- Your prospects will not change their mind.
- Your prospects want the cheapest price.
- Your prospects won't pay in advance.
- Your prospect is not talking to any of your competitors.

The dangerous thing about assumptions is that even though they may be true some of the time, they are often not true all of the time. For example, a salesperson who is selling a premium product and who is poor at qualifying prospects may begin to assume that the price is too high, even though they are making some sales at the correct price.

Making positive assumptions will help improve your sales. For example, assume that your target audience wants help to solve the problems you can fix. Thinking like this will give us the enthusiasm to take action. Assuming that people will like and trust you will help develop good relationships. Even though part of you knows full well that not everyone will want to solve the problem and not everyone will like and trust you, if you act as if they do then more of them will. As long as we build in safeguards to check our positive assumptions, using them proactively can help us boost sales activity and results. Similarly, identifying and challenging our limiting assumptions will also help improve our sales. For example, don't assume that a prospect that does not return your calls is not interested in buying from you.

🗩🗩 COACHING SESSION 89

Consider how you can use assumptions to improve your sales performance.

Positive assumptions that I will now make:

_____

_____

_____

Limiting assumptions I make that I will now challenge:

_____

_____

_____

LIMITING BELIEFS

Beliefs are very similar to assumptions except that they tend to be more deeply ingrained. Beliefs can start as assumptions and the more evidence we get that supports an assumption, the more we convince ourselves it is true and begin to ignore or explain away any evidence to the contrary.

Through experiences and examples we form theories and, once we do, we continue to notice evidence that supports the belief and ignore the evidence that proves the belief to be incorrect. In fact, beliefs are often based on incomplete information and in many cases it is possible to find counter-examples that show the belief to be inaccurate.

Example

Let's say that Sally has got into a role that requires her to sell. Sally seeks advice from three people she knows and believes to be successful in sales and one of the consistent messages she gets back from all three is 'You have got to be pushy to succeed'.

Not knowing any differently, and with three people who she assumes know what they are talking about, combined with many personal experiences of salespeople being pushy, Sally is now certain that she needs to be pushy. This is a problem for Sally because it makes her feel very uncomfortable and this affects her performance. She has taken on a limiting belief.

Developing limiting beliefs that affect our sales is easily done. Like most beliefs, with a bit of research, Sally could easily find plenty of examples which contradict the belief. However, because she trusted the source, she assumed it was true. She now begins to notice other people saying the same thing and that just makes the belief stronger.

Spotting limiting beliefs

Our brains are wired to try to make sense of the world and if we are not careful, our assumptions turn into beliefs that we do not question because we are certain they are true. Some of our most entrenched limiting beliefs may have been formed when we were very young and although they may have protected us at the time, they do not serve us well as adults, especially when it comes to sales. For example:

Belief	Impact on sales
It's rude to talk about money.	In sales situations it is rude to avoid talking about money.
Strangers are dangerous.	In sales, strangers are your friends.
People don't like me.	In sales, people will like you if you help them solve their problems.

It is fairly easy to spot limiting beliefs and assumptions if you know what you are looking for. Many involve the verb 'to be'. For example:

- 'I am too old for sales.'
- 'I can't (i.e. I am unable to) get to speak to Mr Hughes.'
- 'I am not cut out to be in sales.'
- 'I will never (i.e. I am unable to) meet my target!'
- 'Mr Hughes is too busy to take my call.'
- 'Nobody is buying at present.'

COACHING SESSION 90

Complete these sentences.

1. Selling is all about ...

2. All salespeople are ...

3. Money is ...

4. To be successful in sales you need ...

5. My products and services are …

_____

_____

_____

6. My competitors are …

_____

_____

_____

Your answers above will all be beliefs. As you read your answers, consider which of them you think might have a negative impact on your sales results.

Changing limiting beliefs

Changing our limiting beliefs can potentially have a profound impact on our sales performance.

While removing a belief is technically possible, it normally requires the help of a professional. The easier way to deal with a limiting belief is to change the belief by taking the following steps:

1. Begin to doubt the existing belief.

2. Seek evidence to support the doubt.

3. Decide on a more empowering belief.

4. Seek evidence to support the new belief.

5. Reinforce the evidence that supports the new belief.

For example, Gary is an IT consultant and he believes that in order to succeed in sales you need to be an extravert. Gary is an introvert and he provides technical consulting to clients, but his job now requires him to get involved with sales activity. Gary does not bother trying to improve his selling skills because he believes it would be a waste of time since he is 'not cut out for sales', even though his boss sees great potential in Gary.

If Gary were to be tasked with finding examples of introverted IT consultants who were achieving sales success, at some point he would begin to see that introverts can be successful in sales; they just sell in a different way. Perhaps a more empowering belief for Gary would be something like:

'Introverts can be successful in sales if they sell consultatively.'

Each introverted person Gary meets who is successful at consultative selling will help reinforce this belief and make it a more empowering belief for Gary.

Example

Limiting belief	Evidence that contradicts your limiting belief	Empowering alternative	Evidence to support your empowering belief
My prices are too high.	I have customers who have paid the full price. Customers who I have given a discount to have not appreciated the quality.	My ideal customers appreciate they get excellent value for money.	I have asked five existing customers about the value they get. Many customers who originally went with our competitors have come back to us because of the superior quality.

COACHING SESSION 91

Now pick a limiting belief and consider how you can come up with a more empowering belief. You may find it easier to do this session with a colleague or mentor.

Limiting belief	Evidence that contradicts your limiting belief	Empowering alternative	Evidence to support your empowering belief

CHANGING YOUR SELF-TALK

Our mindset and beliefs are greatly influenced by our inner dialogue, also commonly known as self-talk. Inner dialogue is what we say to ourselves. Some people are very aware of their inner dialogue. It is like an internal voice that runs inside our heads as we go about our daily lives. With some people it only runs in certain circumstances and with others it is running all the time. The sound of the self-talk may be the individual's voice or, indeed, the voice of another person such as a parent.

Some people are unaware of their inner dialogue and yet it is probably running just the same. This inner dialogue has an impact on beliefs and assumptions and it is something we should seek to get working for us, rather than against us. A simple way of doing this is through affirmations.

Affirmations are like simple statements that we consciously say to direct our thinking. The statements in the self-assessments at the beginning of each chapter are useful things you can say to yourself over and over again to affirm your mindset in each area of sales. At present, the statement may not be true. However, when you regularly affirm the statement and start acting upon it, you slowly begin to believe the statement and at some point the statement will become true.

There has been a lot written about the power of affirmations and why they work. A good book to read on the subject is *What to Say When You Talk to Yourself* by Shad Helmstetter.

⊕⊕ COACHING SESSION 92

Pick out the top ten statements that you know you need to achieve from the self-assessments at the start of each chapter. Write them down in the spaces below. Transfer them to a card and then repeat them to yourself several times a day while making sure you are acting as if they were true. That means taking the action that you are affirming.

My top 10 affirmations	
Priority	Affirmation
1.	
2.	

3.	
4.	
5.	
6.	
7.	
8.	
9.	
10.	

→ NEXT STEPS

So far in this section we have looked at things that will have an impact on our effectiveness at sales, such as motivation, controlling emotions and our mindset. In the next chapter we will look at another thing that has a huge impact on our sales performance: how we use our time.

TAKEAWAYS

What have I learned?

1. Why is it important to work on developing your sales mindset?

_____

_____

_____

_____

_____

_____

_____

_____

_____

_____

2. How do assumptions and beliefs affect sales performance?

_____

_____

_____

_____

_____

_____

_____

_____

_____

_____

_____

3. What are affirmations and how do they help develop mindset?

16 | PRIORITIZING YOUR SALES ACTIVITY

 OUTCOMES FROM THIS CHAPTER

- Create more time for sales
- Assess the sales potential of a customer account
- Prioritize your account development time

COACHING SESSION 93

Self-assessment

Assessment criteria	Score
I devote as much of my time as possible to revenue-generating activity.	
I take action to eliminate any activity that reduces my time for revenue-generating activity.	
I use a CRM system to track the progress of my sales opportunities.	
I allocate sufficient time to developing customer accounts.	
I prioritize the time I spend with customer accounts based on sales growth potential.	
TOTAL	

Score yourself between 1 and 5. A score of 5 means this statement is totally true; 1 means this statement is totally untrue. Total up your score. The maximum is 25 out of 25. Even if you give yourself a full score, I recommend you complete this chapter.

TIME IS MONEY

The time we have available for sales is limited and to improve our sales performance we need to find ways of becoming more productive with our time. I would like you to start thinking in terms of your time being an investment in the same way as you might invest your money: you want to get a return on your time invested.

The first step to increasing the return you get on your sales time is to review how you currently allocate your time during your working day. Some tasks will have a direct impact on sales while others, like admin tasks, need to be done but are unlikely to have a direct impact. We want to be maximizing the amount of time we have on important sales tasks. The other tasks may still need to be done but we may be able to find a way of reducing the time they take.

Keeping timesheets for a period of time can help to identify many small pockets of time wasted that can be reclaimed.

Example

Derek reviews how he is spending his time and he notices that he is spending a lot of time travelling to and from customers and prospects. He also spends quite a bit of time on administrative tasks. By switching to travelling by train he is now able to use some of his travel time to do administrative tasks.

COACHING SESSION 94

In a spreadsheet, keep a time diary for a week, writing down what tasks you are doing during each 15-minute period of your working day. Once you have finished, create some task categories. For example:

1. Research

2. Lead generation (including leads from existing accounts)

3. Qualifying

4. Discovery meetings

5. Writing proposals

6. Negotiating sales opportunities

7. Relationship building (including networking)

8. Account management (including account reviews and sorting out problems)

9. Travel

10. Admin

11. Updating CRM

12 Non-sales-related admin

13 Other

At the end of the week, go through your list and apply a category to each item in your list and then start totalling each category. Once you have done that, enter the details below, making sure you are accounting for at least 80 per cent of your time during the week.

Category	Total time (hrs)	%
TOTAL TIME		100%

Now that you have an idea of how you are spending or investing your time, consider what you can do to release more time to invest in activity that will create more time.

MANAGING SALES OPPORTUNITIES

When used properly, a customer relationship management system (CRM) can save us a lot of time because it can help prioritize our sales activity and we can keep all information about specific sales opportunities and customer accounts in one place. We can organize our sales activity and record the results so that when we contact customers in the future we can easily recall the details of previous conversations and what was agreed.

From a sales perspective, CRM systems are very useful for managing our sales opportunities, helping us to reach our sales targets and improving our sales conversion rates. Most CRM systems allow you to track the progress of your sales opportunities as they progress through your sales process. This may not seem significant when you look at an individual sales opportunity. Collectively, however, it helps us to see how we are progressing towards our sales targets, especially when we put in additional information such as the expected value and the expected close date. This collective view of sales opportunities is commonly referred to as a 'sales pipeline' because it indicates that the value of sales revenue on its way.

Regularly reviewing your sales pipeline against your sales targets can focus your attention on what needs to be done in order to reach your sales target.

REVIEW YOUR CUSTOMERS' POST-SALES EXPERIENCE

If you find that you are spending a lot of time on resolving customer issues post sales then it is worth getting proactive about reclaiming that time. The first priority is that we have correctly set our customer's expectations prior to the sale and have not sold something that cannot be delivered. If it is an operational issue, it is worth investing some time to seek a resolution to the high issues causing such problems to occur. Depending on your organization, you may need to influence various people to get such matters resolved so that they do not waste your selling time. Consider what you can do during the sales process to minimize complications. For example, you could:

- involve people who are required to deliver what you are selling into your sales process
- ensure that the prospect does whatever they can in advance to make sure the delivery runs smoothly
- qualify out sales opportunities that are likely to cause problems.

A customer is more likely to buy from you again and refer you to their contacts if the post-sales experience matches or is better than their expectations rather than worse! Although there may be some issues that are outside your control, they may still be within your influence. It is up to us to take charge and ensure that things are done to improve the situation.

ACCOUNT MANAGEMENT VS ACCOUNT DEVELOPMENT

You may have discovered already that it is normally easier to win additional sales from an existing customer than it is to find a new customer and that it takes a lot less time too. If you implement what you have learned so far in this book and focus on your ideal customers, then an increasing number of your sales opportunities should come from existing customers. However, we still need to be spending around 50 per cent of our time finding and developing new customers, unless you are in an account management role. Even then, you need to be spending time nurturing the relationships within the new customer account to lay the foundations for future sales growth. We need to be proactive around managing our interactions with customers so that we can fit it all in.

I find it useful to distinguish between managing existing business (account management) and tasks that involve winning new business (account development). Account management tasks include:

- account reviews
- resolving day-to-day issues
- nurturing relationships
- securing existing business.

Account development, on the other hand, is about expanding an account and it includes tasks such as:

- proactively seeking cross-selling and up-selling opportunities
- proactively expanding useful contacts within the customer account
- proactively seeking internal referrals to new sales opportunities elsewhere in the organization.

The trick is to combine the two so that you are proactively seeking new business opportunities while properly managing the existing business.

COACHING SESSION 95

How much of your time is devoted to growing your customer accounts compared to maintaining accounts?

Tasks	% time
Growing	
Maintaining	
TOTAL	100%

PRIORITIZING YOUR ACCOUNT DEVELOPMENT TIME

Many salespeople use the size of existing revenue as an indicator of where to spend most of their time. This is understandable because you want to safeguard existing sales and protect them from competitors. However, some of the smaller-sized accounts could have much more potential for sales growth.

The 5 Star customer exercise we did in Chapter 1 (coaching session 4) should give you an indication of sales growth potential. The more stars a customer has, the better the fit to our organization. Potential customers with zero stars could appear to have lots of sales potential. However, because the fit to our organization is not good, we could waste a lot of time post sales trying to realize that sales potential. It is much better to focus on customers who are going to be the source of additional sales and take us less time and effort to achieve those sales.

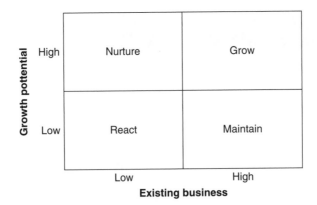

In the matrix above, you can see that existing business has been plotted against growth potential. Some of your customer accounts may have high existing sales and yet little potential for sales growth. In such cases they should continue to be maintained. There is no point in trying to grow an account that has reached its full potential and you should be focused on defending it against the competition.

A customer account that has a high sales growth potential but is undeveloped should be nurtured. This means focusing on building solid, trusted relationships with influential people within the account. You are still looking for sales opportunities, but you should be playing for the long term. However, once you have built the trusted relationships, you should find that sales opportunities become more frequent and easier to win. When this happens then it signifies that the customer account is ready for fast and significant short-term sales growth. Your account development activity, therefore, should be prioritized between nurturing, growing and maintaining.

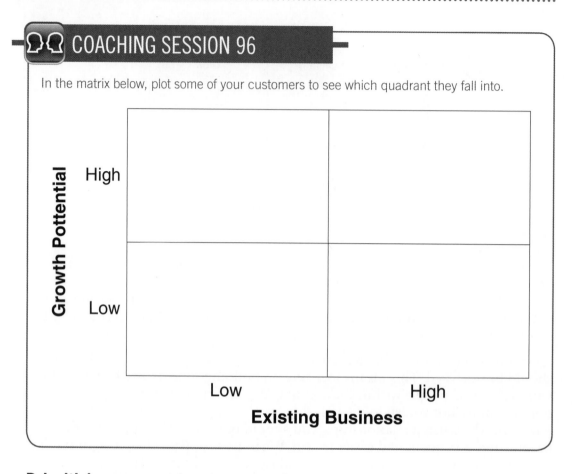

COACHING SESSION 96

In the matrix below, plot some of your customers to see which quadrant they fall into.

Prioritizing your customer accounts

The 5 Star criteria (see Chapter 1) should be the first element of prioritization. The purpose of the 5 Star criteria is to identify the qualities of an ideal customer. If done correctly, then the more stars a customer has, the better fit they have with your organization and consequently the more likely they will need additional products and services.

However, against the 5 Star criteria, we need to assess the growth potential of the customer account. Size of the customer organization will not always be the best indicator of sales potential. It is easy to assume that a major international corporation with a massive budget will have more potential than a medium-sized national organization. The question should not be 'How big is their annual budget?' It should be about how much of their annual budget they are likely to spend with you.

For example, a small consulting firm may win some training business with a large corporation looking for specialist expertise. While the large corporation may have a large annual training budget, they may prefer to deal with just one training organization that can deliver the training across the world in multiple languages. In such circumstances, the growth potential for the consulting firm may be lower than with a medium-sized organization that is seeking a much fuller service and has the potential for follow-on consulting services.

The method I like to use in prioritizing customer accounts is to split them into three categories: Rocks, Pebbles and Sand. The names come from the chapter on prioritization in Stephen R. Covey's book *The 7 Habits of Highly Effective People*: 'Put first things first'. The habit is about prioritizing activities and he uses an analogy of fitting Rocks, Pebble and Sand into a pint glass. He tells the story of a university professor showing the students how it is impossible to fit his collection of rocks, pebbles and sand all into the same pint glass by putting in the sand first, then the pebbles, followed by the rocks. However, he goes on to show them that it *is* possible if you first put the rocks into the glass. Then you can fit the pebbles into the gaps between the rocks. The sand then fits into the gaps between the pebbles and the rocks.

The purpose of the analogy is to get us focusing our attention on our 'rock' activities and, around those activities, fit in our pebble activities. The sand activity can then fit in between the pebbles and the rocks. So, from a sales perspective, we need to be clear what category of customer account we are dealing with.

Sand accounts are normally relatively easy to win but have a limited sales growth potential. Rocks, on the other hand, have a large sales growth potential but take more time and effort to win and nurture. If we were to spend time only on sand-type accounts because they are easy, our sales would plateau because of their limited sales growth potential. On the other hand, if we focused only on accounts with a very large sales growth potential, we might have to wait a long time before we started winning sufficient sales. Just like the analogy, we should focus our activity on the rocks but be careful to do sufficient sales activity with the pebbles and sand for the 'bread and butter' sales.

For example, while we may not make a long journey just to visit a sand prospect, if we can combine it with visiting a rock or pebble account in the area then it may become more viable. Whenever we do go and visit rock and pebble accounts, we should be looking to see whether we can add in any new business activity with sand accounts and prospects in the area. At the end of the day, it is a judgement call as to how to use your limited time and how you can maximize your return on time invested.

Example

Here is an example of rock, pebble and sand accounts for one of my sales coaching customers:

Type	Potential annual sales
Rocks	Greater than £250,000+
Pebbles	Between £100,000 and £250,000
Sand	Between £50,000 and £100,000

With this particular example, if they do not believe that a potential customer will be able to achieve minimum annual sales of £50,000 within three years then they will not even do business with them. It is the quality in their 5 Star criteria that is non-negotiable because they want to ensure that the sales effort will result in recurring and growing annual sales revenue.

COACHING SESSION 97

Specify the criteria for your rock, pebble and sand accounts:

Type	Potential annual sales	Comments
Rocks		
Pebbles		
Sand		

NEXT STEPS

Sales is a people business and the last area we will be looking at in terms of increasing sales performance is in improving our effectiveness when dealing with people.

TAKEAWAYS

What have I learned?

1. Why is it important to review how you are currently spending your time?

_____

_____

_____

_____

_____

_____

_____

_____

_____

_____

2. What is the difference between account management and account development?

_____

_____

_____

_____

_____

_____

_____

_____

_____

_____

_____

3. What are two ways of determining the growth potential of customer accounts?

IMPROVING YOUR SKILL WITH PEOPLE

✔ OUTCOMES FROM THIS CHAPTER

- Easily gain rapport with prospects and customers
- Know the number-one selling skill and how to develop it
- Understand the importance of speaking your customers' language

COACHING SESSION 98

Self-assessment

Assessment criteria	Score
I like people and take an interest in them.	
I take time to develop rapport whenever I meet people.	
I always seek to understand my customers' perspective before communicating my sales messages.	
I am careful to ensure that the meaning of my communication is correctly understood by customers and prospects.	
I take care to remain credible with customers and prospects and I always deliver on my promises.	
TOTAL	

Score yourself between 1 and 5. A score of 5 means this statement is totally true; 1 means this statement is totally untrue. Total up your score. The maximum is 25 out of 25. Even if you give yourself a full score, I recommend you complete this chapter.

SELLING IS A PEOPLE GAME

Whatever you are selling, it is impossible to avoid people. Even for businesses that sell products and services on the Internet without actually having to interact with anyone directly, you still have to consider how to engage and interact with people through websites, sales landing pages and email. A big transformation in selling skill normally happens when the salesperson starts to pay more attention to understanding the world of their customers rather than just focusing on their own sales targets. Sales should be something we do *with* customers rather than being a battle fought against customers.

Sales is hard work unless you like people. Somehow people can tell if you are only interested in their money. It tends to show through body language, the way we speak or the words we choose. It does not matter how good our selling skills are or how motivated we feel; if people do not like and trust us then they are unlikely to consider doing business with us.

GAINING RAPPORT

Did you ever have a sales meeting where your prospective customer seemed very 'frosty' and kept you at arm's length? And have you had sales meetings with people who seem very relaxed and open to listening to what you have to say? The difference will be rapport. If you want to develop and nurture business relationships then you need to spend time developing rapport with people before getting down to business. Rapport makes communication and trust easier to develop because during the process of rapport we lower our guard and get on to each other's wavelength. Once we have rapport, communication becomes much easier and more relaxed.

Rapport is a naturally existing state between humans and when we have rapport we tend to match our body language and words. Many books on people skills tell you that if you start to match the other person's body language then it is possible to get into rapport with the other person. You can also match voice tone and words. Other books will tell you that instead of matching body language you should 'mirror' their body language, meaning that you do something similar but not identical. For example, if they scratch their nose then you scratch your ear. The problem is that unless you are sincerely interested in the other person then, in my experience, matching and mirroring rarely works. Moreover, if you take an interest in the other person and sincerely seek to find things in common then you will find that rapport happens naturally anyway without you having to try.

The easiest way to gain rapport is through small talk. It is something we do naturally in a social context but sometimes forget to do in a sales context. Get the other person to talk about something they are interested in – themselves! If you have never met them before then you might ask them how long they have been in their role and what they were doing previously. You could ask whether they live locally or have to travel far into work. You could even comment on the working environment and if you are very desperate you can start talking about the weather! Imagine you are at your best friend's party and you are introduced to a friend of your friend. If the other person sees you as a friendly person who is interested in them and what they have to say then they will begin to lower their guard and provide you with the information you need for sales purposes.

COACHING SESSION 99

In your next discovery meeting, pay attention to developing rapport with your prospective customer. What signs did you have that you achieved rapport? If you did not achieve rapport, what will you do differently next time?

Prospective customer	Signs of rapport	What I will do differently
1.		
2.		
3.		
4.		
5.		
6.		

SEEING THINGS FROM YOUR CUSTOMER'S PERSPECTIVE

Habit number 5 In Stephen R. Covey's excellent book *The 7 Habits of Highly Effective people* is 'Seek first to understand, then to be understood'. In my view, this is the most important skill in consultative selling because it underpins everything.

- When we understand our target audience's problems, we can get a sense of their potential motives for wanting to have a sales conversation with us.

- When a prospective customer is interested in a sales conversation then we need to discover their problem in more depth so that we can come up with a solution.

- When we make a proposal we need to use our understanding to pitch our solution.

- The more we anticipate a prospective customer's issues, the less likely it is that we are going to need to overcome objections.

- In the event that we do need to negotiate the solution with a prospective customer, we need to be able to see things from the prospective customer's perspective in order to come to a win-win deal.

- And the more we anticipate our customer's additional needs and wants, the easier it will be to gain additional sales from them.

The first stage to understanding your prospective customers is to ask good open questions so that they tell us what is on their mind. However, the big leap forward comes when we start to imagine what their world is like and begin to see the world through their eyes. When we do this, we begin to understand what is driving their behaviour along with their concerns and preferences. This in turn allows us to modify our own behaviour and communication to maximize our influence.

There are a number of techniques for seeing things from your customer's perspective. The simplest is a technique I call 'Customer Hats', which is based on Edward de Bono's work *Six Thinking Hats*. In de Bono's work you change your perspective on a problem based on the colour and purpose of the hat you are wearing. For example, when you are wearing the yellow hat you approach a problem with optimism. Changing the hat to, say, green, you now switch to thinking about the problem creatively, and with the black hat you start to think in terms of 'devil's advocate' and take a negative point of view. When you think of the problem from all six viewpoints you get a fuller picture and from there you are able to make better decisions.

With Customer Hats, you actually have one hat which is your salesperson hat. When you are wearing your salesperson's hat you can be as selfish and target focused as you like. However, once you put on your customer hat, you can only see things from their perspective. You would say to yourself something like 'putting on my customer hat ...' You then start writing or speaking as if you were the customer and as a result you often will gain additional insights which you can use when you are back to being a salesperson!

Customer hats can be useful for seeing things generically from your target audience's perspective. You imagine being a typical customer and review your proposed communication as if you were one of them. It is even more powerful if you have a special hat for a specific customer or prospect. If you find it hard to imagine a hat then why not get a physical hat to represent customer thinking?

COACHING SESSION 100

Imagine a customer hat that you can wear when seeing things from a customer's perspective.

- What type of hat is it?
- What colour is it?

Now imagine a hat that represents you as a salesperson.

- What type of hat is it?
- What colour is it?

Focusing on a specific customer-related problem such as a prospective customer who is not returning your calls … write down your observations from your own perspective and the perspective of the customer. Then note down your insights and how you will use them in the future.

My perspective on the problem	
My customer's perspective on the problem	
Insights gained	
How I will use this insight	

SPEAKING OUR CUSTOMER'S LANGUAGE

Gaining rapport with our customers and seeing things from their perspective is a good start, but we need to be effective at communicating with them if we want to be able to influence them and encourage them to see that we are their best option for solving their problems. As humans, everything we do communicates something. Even when we say nothing we are communicating something!

If we were to go to France and try to sell our products and services, we could decide to just sell to those who could speak English. If we wanted to reach more people then we would have to learn to speak French or rely on an interpreter and risk things being lost in translation. The point is that to raise our game in sales we need to continually work on our communication so that our customers and prospects understand our messages as we intended. We all have subtle differences in the way we communicate and process information and it's safe to assume that buyers will not put in a lot of effort to adapt their communication style. They will expect the salesperson to make the effort to be understood. Therefore we need to get good at adapting our communication style.

COMMON COMMUNICATION MISTAKES

Slang

People from different regions and countries could use different words to mean the same thing and they could also use local slang. We need to make sure we are using global words that can easily be understood, especially if communicating with people from another country where English is not their first language. We need to be using the kind of words that someone who has studied business English is likely to understand.

Pronunciation

As well as using words that the other person is likely to understand, we need to be sure that we articulate our words clearly and speak at a speed we can be sure the other person can understand. English is normally spoken at around 150 words per minute and if you are speaking to someone who is not fluent at English then you may need to slow it down slightly to between 100 and 120 words per minute.

Jargon

Using jargon is always a bad idea when communicating, unless you know that the other person understands the jargon or you take the time to explain the jargon first. The risk with jargon is that people stop listening while they try to work out what the word means. It is much better to play it safe with easily understandable words or take the time to explain the jargon.

Acronyms

Abbreviations and acronyms have a similar effect to jargon. We tend to use these as shorthand, not realizing that not everyone knows the same shorthand.

When we say UK instead of United Kingdom or USA instead of United States of America, most people will know what we are talking about. However, if we are going to use an acronym or abbreviation, we need to first establish the meaning of the abbreviation. Also, when writing emails, we need to use proper words rather than shortening them or abbreviating them, as we may do when sending a personal message to a close friend.

Ambiguity

Unless we are careful, our communication can be interpreted in more than one way. For example, consider this simple sentence:

'Please send me a copy.'

It may seem perfectly straightforward but actually there are two potentially ambiguous words:

- 'Copy' – Is that a physical copy or a soft copy?
- 'Send' – How, specifically, is it to be sent?

In addition to that there is an ambiguity around when the copy is required.

The important thing is that we take care to ensure that what we communicate is likely to be understood the way we want it to be.

⊕⊕ COACHING SESSION 101

Which of the following mistakes do you recognize in your own communication?

Mistake	Tick
Slang	
Unclear pronunciation	
Jargon	
Acronyms	
Ambiguity	

COMMUNICATING TRUST

Throughout this book, a common theme is that gaining the trust of customers is a critical element of sales success. Prospective customers start evaluating whether they trust us from the very moment we first meet. Indeed, with the Internet and social media, they could already have formed an opinion of you and your company from a Google search. There are three significant aspects of communication that will help us accelerate trust with prospective customers.

Firstly, we need to recognize that our body language and voice tone play an important part in effective communication and the words we use need to match our body language. Indeed, people will typically pay more attention to the non-verbal elements of communication. This is hard to fake unless you are a good actor. The simplest way to ensure that your communication is fully integrated is to be open and honest – in other words, to sell with integrity.

Secondly, we need to be careful in our communication that our claims about our products and services are credible. We need to take care that what we say sounds plausible and sometimes that may mean understating the impact of our products and services.

Finally, we need to be careful in our communication to correctly set expectations. Many prospective customers will look at whether you follow through with your promises. Consistently promising things and not delivering them runs the risk of your being interpreted as someone whose word cannot be trusted. It can be the small things that matter such as turning up to meetings on time or returning a call at the agreed time.

 NEXT STEPS

This is the end of the book and if you have not completed all the other chapters it is worth going through them just to see whether you can pick up one or two additional insights. You may also want to redo some of the chapters which you previously found challenging, once you have had a chance to implement what you have learned.

TAKEAWAYS

What have I learned?

1. Why is rapport important in sales? And what is a simple method of achieving rapport with customers and prospects?

_____

_____

_____

_____

_____

_____

_____

_____

_____

2. What is the number one selling skill? And what is a method for developing this skill?

_____

_____

_____

_____

_____

_____

_____

_____

_____

_____

3. What are three of the communication mistakes to be avoided? And why are they a
   problem?

PROGRESS CHART

Measure	Baseline	Month 1	Month 2	Month 3
New customers:				
Number of leads generated				
Lead quality % (proportion of sales leads not qualified out)				
Value of proposals delivered (your sales pipeline)				
Number of sales won				
Average value of sales won				
Average conversion % (leads converted into sales)				
Average sales cycle (time taken to close the sale)				
Existing customers:				
Number of leads generated				
Lead quality % (proportion of sales leads not qualified out)				
Value of proposals delivered (your sales pipeline)				
Number of sales won				
Average value of sales won				
Average conversion % (leads converted into sales)				
Average sales cycle (time taken to close the sale)				

BIBLIOGRAPHY AND REFERENCES

Alessandra, T., *Non-manipulative Selling* (Fireside, 1992)

Bosworth, M., *Solution Selling* (McGraw-Hill, 1995)

Carnegie, D., *How to Win Friends and Influence People* (Simon & Schuster, 1981)

Cathcart, J., *Relationship Selling* (Perigee, 1990)

Connor, T., *Soft Sell* (Sourcebooks, 1994)

Covey, S., *The 7 Habits of Highly Effective People* (Simon & Schuster, 1992)

Galper, Ari, *Unlock the Game.* Online course with respect to cold calling www.unlockthegame.com

Giblin, L., *How to Have Confidence and Power in Dealing with People* (Prentice Hall, 1956)

Godin, S., *All Marketers are Liars* (Penguin Books, 2007)

Heath, D. and Heath, C., *Made to Stick* (Arrow Books, 2008)

Helmstetter, S., *What to Say When You Talk to Yourself* (Thorsons, 1991)

Jenkins, D. and Gregory J., *The Gorillas Want Bananas* (Lean Marketing Press, 2008)

Knight, S., *NLP at Work* (Nicholas Brealey Publishing, 1992)

Maister, D., Green C. and Galford, R., *The Trusted Advisor* (Simon & Schuster, 2002)

Malz, M., Kennedy, D. et al., *Zero-Resistance Selling* (Prentice Hall, 1998)

Matthews, A., *Making Friends* (Media Masters, 1990)

Miller, R. and Heiman, S., *The New Conceptual Selling* (Kogan Page, 2011)

Miller, R. and Heiman, S., *The New Strategic Selling* (Kogan Page, 2011)

Misner, I. and Davis, R., *Business by Referral* (Bard Press, 1998)

Misner, I. and Morgan, D., *Masters of Networking* (Bard Press, 2000)

O'Connor, J. and Prior, R., *Successful Selling with NLP* (Thorsons, 2000)

Rackham, N., *SPIN Selling* (McGraw-Hill, Random House, 1988)

Robbins, R., *Awaken the Giant Within* (Pocket Books, 1992)

Robbins, R., *Unlimited Power* (Simon & Schuster, 1989)

Southon, M. and West, C., *Sales on a Beermat* (Random House, 2005)

Tracy, B., *The Psychology of Selling* (Audio CD) (Nightingale Conant, 1995)

White, R., *Consultative Selling For Professional Services* (CreateSpace, 2014)

White, R., *The Accidental Salesman Networking Survival Guide* (bookshaker.com, 2011)

INDEX

28/02/15